SELF-ESTEEM FOR TEENS

Mastering Self-Love and Building Limitless Confidence

A Proven Path to Transform Your Life
and Achieve Your Dreams

The Mentor Bucket

CONTENTS

INTRODUCTION

Do you feel you're unloved and unwanted by every-one around you? Do you avoid new things and seldom take advantage of opportunities? Do you tend to blame others for your mistakes?

If you've always had difficulty making friends, engaged in negative self-talk that makes you compare yourself to others, been scared to stand in front of people, and been unable to accept compliments without showing mixed feelings of anxiety or stress, then you're likely dealing with low self-esteem and lack of confidence. As you search for your place in the world, you face situations that challenge your beliefs about yourself.

While it can be normal for teenagers to lack confidence sometimes, it's not normal when this is constant. People with self-esteem and confidence issues see themselves differently from the way others see them.

When I was dealing with low self-esteem and lack of con-fidence, I avoided situations where I saw a risk of failure, mistakes, and possible embarrassment. These situations involved making friends, doing schoolwork, and trying new activities, which are all important features of a healthy teenage life.

I remember always having a smile on my face to please the people around me while knowing it was a façade. I always used negative self-talk to pull myself down whenever I felt like I wasn't good enough. It became hard for me to deal with normal levels of frustration, and I always felt as if no one wanted or loved me.

Even when I got positive feedback in school, I always had issues accepting it because I'd question my abilities by thinking, *"Am I that good?"* After dealing with the effects of low self-esteem and lack of self-confidence for a long time, I finally admitted that I needed help. That decision changed my life for the better.

Like me, you probably have been dealing with low self-esteem and a lack of self-confidence. We've all been there at some point in our lives, when it feels like we aren't confident in our abilities to get things right. Each day as we wake up, we feel like staying in our beds and not getting up because we aren't motivated to see people and face the challenges of each day. However, that mental state isn't ideal for *anyone*.

When we don't renounce that mental state, it leads to problems such as constantly experiencing negative moods, which can include sadness, anxiety, shame, anger, difficulty making friends, decreased motivation, poor body image, abuse, etc.

The teenage years can sometimes be stressful and awkward. Teens who seem confident in childhood may struggle with maintaining their self-esteem and confidence during their teenage years. This could be due to insecurity, self-doubt, or a questionable body image. When you look at the advent of social media and technology, your self-esteem and confidence can suffer even more. You will see your self-esteem flickering and waning like a candle, making it crucial to arm yourself with strategies that can work against the effects.

Researchers say poor self-esteem and lack of confidence are directly linked to mental health issues. Due to the invisible developments in a teenager's brain, self-esteem and confidence can be ignited or they can be extinguished, which leads to possible detrimental consequences.

Teen cognitive abilities that aren't related to self-regulation aren't well developed. As a result, teenagers tend to take risks. They often react emotionally instead of logically. With the brain development that happens during the teenage years, teens have difficulty managing their emotions. They prefer to bottle up their emotions inside rather than talk about them, which can lead to damaging outcomes.

The good news is that you can build a strong sense of your worth and value. With this book, you can take the right steps to build your self-esteem and improve your confidence. When you achieve this, you'll be better prepared to navigate challenges, handle peer pressure, make better decisions, and recover from setbacks.

For many years, I've been passionate about helping kids flourish during their intensely transformative years. Luckily, I've had the opportunity to speak directly with teens in schools about bullying, substance abuse prevention, peer pressure, and the coping skills needed to find their grit, build resiliency, and navigate intense emotions. The goal is to help teens build positive self-esteem and confidence.

Positive self-esteem is important as it allows you to take risks, try new things, and solve problems. As a result, your learning and growth will be productive, transforming your life.

When you're confident in yourself and your abilities, and you have healthy self-esteem, you will likely display positive behavioral characteristics such as taking pride in your accomplishments, acting more maturely and independently, accepting that you're frustrated and dealing with that responsibly, loving yourself, helping others in need, and trying out new challenges and experiences.

This book is a result of my research and personal experience concerning the impact of low self-esteem and lack of confidence on a teen's life. Knowing these effects are damaging, I want to see you rise above them and fight for your mental health by building your self-esteem and confidence.

This is a straightforward book that provides a proven approach you can use to transform your life and achieve your dreams. With the effective and result-driven ideas you'll find here, you can empower yourself to eliminate feelings of low self-esteem and build your confidence. After reading, you can start implementing all you've learned.

To tackle an issue, we need to understand it; therefore, we'll kickstart our journey with the first chapter where I'll discuss the concept of self-esteem and confidence.

Ready for this exciting journey? Let's get started!

CHAPTER 1:
UNDERSTANDING
SELF-ESTEEM AND CONFIDENCE

Self-esteem will help you believe in yourself, overcome obstacles, and achieve your goals. With confidence and the right amount of self-esteem, you can do anything you set your mind on!

I have always loved to play basketball. During the weekend, I would play basketball with my friends for hours. I had a great jump shot and was one of the best players on the team despite being far shorter than the boys on my team.

There was a time when my team was playing a championship game. We were down by two points with only a few seconds left. I knew I was the best option to take the final shot, but I started to doubt myself. I thought, *"I'm too short for making this shot. I'm not good enough."*

Just then, there was a timeout. My coach called me aside and gave me a pep talk. He reminded me of all the hard work I had put in and all the times I had made that same shot in practice. He told me to be confident and trust my abilities.

Guess what! I took the shot and made it! My team won the game, and everyone was cheering and celebrating. Only then did I realize how important confidence and self-esteem were to me. If I hadn't believed in myself, I might have missed that shot, and my team would have lost the game.

This is an introductory chapter that will focus on building the right foundation in this exciting journey of ours. Building the foundation entails knowing what self-esteem and confidence mean. So, let's start with self-esteem.

What is Self-Esteem?

Self-esteem is the way you view yourself. It is how you perceive and evaluate yourself, your abilities, qualities, and overall sense of self-worth. A teen with high self-esteem will be happy and confident because healthy self-esteem is vital for overall well-being and happiness.

Self-esteem can develop from a variety of factors. It could be from your experiences, relationships, and the messages you receive from the world around you. During childhood, we often form our first beliefs about ourselves based on our interactions with our parents and other significant people.

We're more likely to develop a positive sense of self if we receive consistent messages of love, acceptance, and encouragement. However, if we experience neglect, criticism, or abuse, this can damage our self-esteem and lead to negative beliefs about ourselves.

In addition to our early experiences, our self-esteem can be influenced by what we achieve, our successes, our social skills, and our ability to cope with challenges and setbacks. If we achieve our goals and receive positive feedback from others, that can boost our self-esteem. However, comparing ourselves unfavorably to others and being rejected consistently can lower our self-esteem.

High self-esteem means you have a positive view of yourself. You believe in your abilities and have confidence in your decisions and actions. On the other hand, low self-esteem can make you feel inadequate, insecure, and unsure of yourself. It can lead to negative self-talk, self-doubt, and self-criticism, all of which affect your mental health and relationships with others.

Characteristics of People with Low Self-Esteem

Now that you understand the meaning of self-esteem and how it develops, let's explore some common characteristics of people with low self-esteem.

The symptoms of low self-esteem are usually mistaken for signs of fear or anxiety. But there are striking signs that show that you have low self-esteem. They are:

Negative Self-Talk

One of the main characteristics of low self-esteem is engaging in negative self-talk, which is when teens criticize themselves and focus on their weaknesses rather than their strengths. They might think, *"I'm not good enough,"* *"I'm a failure,"* or *"I'm not smart enough."*

Negative self-talk can damage one's mental health and lead to a cycle of low self-esteem and self-doubt.

Difficulty Accepting Compliments

Teens with low self-esteem may have difficulty accepting compliments or praise from others. They may feel that they don't deserve the compliment or that the person giving it is insincere. Instead of feeling good about themselves, they might feel embarrassed or uncomfortable when someone says something positive about them.

Perfectionism

Another common characteristic of teens with low self-esteem is that they always strive for perfectionism. They set high standards for themselves and are critical when they fail to meet them. They might feel they need to be perfect and may have difficulty accepting anything less than that. This can be exhausting and lead to feelings of inadequacy.

People-Pleasing

Teens with low self-esteem are people-pleasers. They go above and beyond, doing things so others will like them.

They often desire to please others even at their own expense. They might say "yes" to things they don't want to do, or they may compromise their values to fit in with others. This can lead to a feeling of being taken advantage of or unappreciated, which contributes to low self-esteem.

Comparing Themselves to Others

Teens with low self-esteem may compare themselves to others and feel they don't measure up. They might think that other people are better looking, more successful, or happier than they are, which can lead to feelings of envy or jealousy. This constant comparison can be exhausting and contribute to low self-esteem.

Fear of Failure

The fear of failure can hold back teens with low self-esteem from trying new things or taking risks. They might think that if they fail, it will confirm their negative beliefs about themselves. This fear can contribute to feelings of low self-esteem by preventing the teen from reaching their full potential.

Negative Body Image

Negative body image is a constant characteristic associated with teens with low self-esteem. They don't like how they look, so they might focus on their flaws and feel self-conscious about their appearance. This can lead to avoiding social situations or feeling uncomfortable in their skin.

Social Withdrawal

When teens start withdrawing from social situations, preferring to be alone rather than around others, they might suffer from low self-esteem. They might feel like they fail to fit in or need to be more interesting to be around. This can lead to loneliness and isolation, which contribute to low self-esteem.

Difficulty Making Decisions

Teens with low self-esteem may have difficulty making decisions, especially when they are focused on themselves and their future. They might feel like they still need to figure out what they want or that they don't yet have the skills or abilities to make the right decision. This can lead to feeling stuck or indecisive and contributes to low self-esteem.

Dependence on External Validation

When teens rely heavily on external validation from others to feel good about themselves, they might experience low self-esteem. They may seek approval or praise from others and feel devastated by criticism or rejection. This can be a fragile foundation for self-esteem, leading to a constant need for validation and a fear of disapproval.

Causes of Low Self-Esteem

Low self-esteem is a common issue among teenagers, and it can cause many problems. It can affect your relationships, academic performance, and overall happiness. However, low self-esteem doesn't just happen! It can be caused by different factors, such as:

- Negative self-talk
- Social media
- Bullying
- Trauma
- Parental influence
- Physical appearance
- Academic performance

What is Self-Confidence?

I used to be very shy and introverted in my teenage years. I always struggled to make friends and speak up in class.

There was one time when we held a talent show at my school; I was asked if I wanted to participate. I have always loved singing but was too afraid to sing in front of others. However, with the encouragement of my family and some friends, I tried it.

I got up on stage and began to sing. At first, my voice was low and shaky, but soon, as I continued to sing, I wasn't scared anymore. I began to stand up straighter, smile, and sing louder. By the song's end, I had the whole audience cheering and applauding me.

After the talent show, I felt a newfound sense of confidence. I realized that I had a talent that I could share with others. This is precisely what self-confidence is all about!

Self-confidence means believing that you're good at what you do. It means feeling good about yourself and your abilities and not being too shy to show others. When you have self-confidence, you trust yourself to handle whatever life throws your way, whether it's a tricky math problem, a sports game, or a social situation.

Self-confidence doesn't mean you never make mistakes or feel unsure about things. It means you have faith in yourself to learn and grow from those experiences. It's like having a solid foundation that allows you to take risks and try new things without worrying too much about what other people think.

Having self-confidence can make a big difference in your life. It can help you feel happier and more fulfilled, make better decisions, and build better relationships.

So, it's essential to work on developing your self-confidence, whether that's through practicing new skills, getting involved in activities you enjoy, or learning to think positively about yourself. When you believe in yourself, others will believe in you too.

Where Does Self-Confidence Come From?

As a teen, you may face many new experiences and challenges that can make you feel unsure of yourself. That's completely normal, and building self-confidence is a process that takes time and practice. So where does self-confidence come from?

Well, the answer is both simple and complex. Self-confidence comes from a variety of sources, including your experiences, your achievements, your relationships, and your mindset. Let's take a closer look at each of these factors.

Experiences

Your experiences shape who you are and what you believe about yourself. Positive experiences can help you build confidence, while negative experiences can erode it.

For example, if you try something new and succeed, you'll feel good about yourself and your abilities. This positive experience can help you feel more confident in trying new things. On the other hand, failing at something or having a negative experience can make you doubt yourself and your abilities.

It's important to remember that everyone has positive and negative life experiences. The key is to focus on positive experiences and use them as building blocks for confidence. When you have a negative experience, try to learn from it and use it as an opportunity to grow and improve.

Achievements

Achievements are another vital source of self-confidence. When you achieve something that you've been working toward, it can give you a sense of accomplishment and pride. This, in turn, can boost your confidence and make you feel more capable of achieving other goals.

It's essential to set realistic goals for yourself and celebrate your achievements, no matter how small they may seem. When you achieve a goal, reflect on what you did well and what you can improve upon in the future. This will help you build confidence and develop a growth mindset, which we'll discuss later.

Relationships

Positive relationships with supportive people can help you feel good about yourself and your abilities. On the other hand, negative relationships with people who put you down or make you feel bad about yourself can erode your confidence.

It's important to surround yourself with people who lift and support you. Seek friends and mentors who believe in you and encourage you to pursue your goals. These positive relationships can help you feel more confident and capable of achieving your dreams.

Mindset

Finally, your mindset plays a crucial role in your self-confidence. Your mindset is the collection of beliefs and attitudes you have about yourself and the world around you. You may believe your abilities are fixed and unchangeable if you have a fixed mindset. This can make you feel stuck and unable to grow or improve.

On the other hand, if you have a growth mindset, you believe your abilities can be developed through hard work and dedication. This can help you feel more confident in learning and growing.

To develop a growth mindset, focus on your effort and progress rather than your results. Instead of focusing on whether you succeeded or failed, think about what you learned from the experience and how you can use that knowledge to improve.

Causes of Low Self-Confidence

Self-confidence is good because it enables you to take on new challenges, pursue your goals, and handle difficult situations. Unfortunately, many people, especially teenagers, struggle with low self-confidence. This impacts their overall well-being and hinders their success. Here are some of the causes of low self-confidence.

- Negative self-talk
- Comparison to others
- Past experiences
- Perfectionism
- Lack of support
- Social media
- Body image

The Thin Line Between Confidence and Arrogance

Confidence and arrogance are two traits that often get mistaken for each other. However, they are not the same thing, and it's essential to understand the difference between them.

Confidence is a positive attribute that helps you believe in yourself and your abilities. It's the ability to trust yourself and your instincts, knowing you can achieve your goals. When you are confident, you feel comfortable in your skin and don't need any external validation to feel good about yourself.

On the other hand, arrogance is a negative trait that often stems from insecurity. It's an overbearing sense of self-importance and a belief that you are superior to others. Arrogant people often put others down to boost their egos and are not open to feedback or criticism.

The thin line between confidence and arrogance lies in how you perceive yourself and treat others. While confidence is a positive trait that can help you achieve your goals, arrogance can hold you back and damage your relationships.

Confident people are humble and open-minded. They don't need to prove themselves to anyone because they trust their abilities. They are willing to learn from others and admit their mistakes, knowing they can improve themselves. Confident people respect others and are eager to listen to their opinions, even if they disagree.

On the other hand, arrogant people are closed-minded and dismissive of others. They believe they are always right, even when, in truth, they need to take feedback or criticism better. They often put others down to boost their ego, and they have difficulty admitting their mistakes. Arrogant people also tend to feel entitled, believing they deserve special treatment or privileges.

Meanwhile, confidence and arrogance also differ in how they impact your relationships. Confident people build solid and positive relationships because they are respectful and open-minded. They are comfortable in their skin, which makes others feel comfortable around them. Confident people inspire others to be their best selves, which helps them build strong, positive relationships.

However, arrogant people often have difficulty building positive relationships because they are dismissive of others. They may come across as condescending or disrespectful, which can push people away. Arrogant people also tend to attract negative attention, making it challenging to build positive relationships.

So, how can you tell the difference between confidence and arrogance? Here are a few signs to look for:

Confidence:

- Believing in yourself and your abilities
- Being open-minded and willing to learn from others
- Being comfortable in your skin
- Respecting others and their opinions
- Inspiring others to be their best selves

Arrogance:

- Believing you are always right
- Dismissing others and their opinions
- Putting others down to boost your ego
- Having a sense of entitlement
- Attracting negative attention

If you want to be confident without crossing over into arrogance, here are a few tips:

- *Believe in yourself*: You must trust your abilities and have confidence. When you believe in yourself, you'll be more likely to take risks and pursue your goals.
- *Stay humble*: Remember that you don't know everything, and there is always room for improvement. Stay open-minded and willing to learn from others.

- *Be respectful*: Treat others respectfully and kindly, even if you disagree with them. Remember that everyone has a unique perspective and experience.
- *Listen to feedback*: Be willing to listen to feedback and criticism and use it to improve yourself. Don't take criticism personally; see it as an opportunity to grow.

CHAPTER 2:
IMPORTANCE OF SELF-ESTEEM
AND CONFIDENCE IN A TEEN'S LIFE

Regardless of your experience, you must understand that you're intrinsically valuable; you are special and worthy of everything good, even when you make mistakes. When you have a good sense of self-esteem and confidence in your abilities, that doesn't suggest you think you're better than others. It shows that you know your strengths and weaknesses, accept them as part of being human, and strive to improve.

Sadly, many teens don't feel good about themselves. They are so fixated on how their imperfections, flaws, and weaknesses affect how they view themselves. Perhaps, you've experienced rejection, abandonment, betrayal, abuse, and negative influence, causing you to fall into the same category as these people.

It would be best to start rebuilding your self-esteem and self-worth because they are keys to transforming your life and achieving your dreams.

Earlier, we discussed the concepts "self-esteem and self-confidence," their causes, and how you shouldn't confuse confidence and arrogance. This chapter will build on what we've discussed in the first chapter by exploring the importance of healthy self-esteem and confidence in your life.

Why Do We Need a Healthy Level of Self-Esteem and Confidence?

Self-esteem is how you perceive your worth and value. It's also your satisfaction or dissatisfaction after exerting your sense of worth. Your self-esteem is essential because it significantly impacts the choices you make as an individual and the decisions you choose to take or reject.

Your self-esteem is the driving force that propels you to harness your capabilities and strive to bring them into play. High self-esteem drives you to do all it takes to preserve your health. You will appreciate that a healthy body is necessary to explore your full capabilities. Besides your physical health, you will be concerned about your mental and psychological well-being. You will be concerned about your happiness and do everything to maintain it.

On the other hand, low self-esteem will make you lose interest in even the essential things, as you will lack the willpower to want to explore your potential or try to achieve anything. Low self-esteem will make you feel unworthy of pursuing your happiness. It will cause you to neglect your physical health as well.

The concept of self-esteem is abstract. It may be difficult for you to understand what it's like to have self-esteem if you don't already have it. For instance, how can you appreciate the feeling of high self-esteem if the level of your current self-esteem is low? The only way around this is to consider your feelings toward the things that are of value in your life. Ask yourself, *"What matters in my life right now, and how do I perceive those things?"*

To illustrate this better, let's say you like dogs and have one called Rover. Because you like Rover, you spend a lot of time caring for him. You are always very mindful of his nutrition, ensuring he's well-fed. You also don't take Rover's health lightly, as you regularly pay scheduled visits to the vet to ensure Rover is healthy and fit. How about regular walks in the park? You always take advantage of every opportunity whenever it shows up! Remember how you love to show Rover off to your friends whenever they come around?

That clearly describes how high self-esteem works. Rover in the illustration represents you. Your actions depict how you care for Rover and how proud you are of yourself. With a healthy level of self-esteem, you will do everything possible to take care of yourself and make good decisions — ones that will increase your self-worth and not diminish it. When you have a healthy level of confidence, you will be proud of yourself and not be afraid to explore your full potential.

These are different facets of self-esteem:

High self-esteem/low self-esteem

You can measure self-esteem in different ways. One such way is the amount or degree to which it's present in different people. Self-esteem can be high or low; you either have high self-esteem or low self-esteem. The difference between someone with high self-esteem and someone with low self-esteem is not visible to the eyes. You can only see the difference when you compare their thought patterns and how they value themselves.

Self-esteem quality

Also known as proportional self-esteem, this scope of self-esteem is its quality, which differs even among people with high self-esteem. The challenges they have to conquer to arrive at their place of accomplishment vary greatly. While some people feel accomplished after a few challenges, others go through much more to become accomplished. Therefore, their self-esteem is proportional to the number of life obstacles they face and conquer.

Disproportional self-esteem – Overinflated

There are other situations where the high self-esteem of some persons is not directly proportional to what they have accomplished or the hurdles they have had to scale through. Such people think highly of themselves, though they can't precisely say what they have accomplished or what actions they have taken to warrant their thinking this highly of themselves. Instead, they have an entitlement mentality toward their self-worth rather than basing that esteem on any potential they have harnessed. Such entitled self-esteem is accompanied by self-seeking and egotistic behaviors, making it less psychologically healthy than directly proportional self-esteem. You can also describe this unhealthy and disproportional self-esteem as overly inflated.

Disproportional self-esteem – Underinflated

While some persons have unhealthy, overly inflated self-esteem, others have low self-esteem, which you can describe as underinflated. Such persons may have gone through life challenges where they maximized their potential and had achievements they should be proud of.

For that reason, they have the right to high self-esteem. Surprisingly, these people trivialize their accomplishments and see nothing worth celebrating! They find a way to constantly belittle themselves for reasons ranging from obsessive compulsion, depression, anxiety, past abuse, and exploitation.

People with underinflated self-esteem usually set unrealistic and unattainable standards for themselves when it comes to judging their achievements. Of course, they never meet that standard, and this causes emotional distress. Ironically, when you observe such persons from the outside and see they have accomplished so much, you tend to find them worthy and deserving. You will never understand why they think so little of themselves!

Self-esteem and confidence are more complex than simply terming them "high" or "low." It doesn't suffice to have high self-esteem, as it also has to be at a healthy level. Suppose you have low self-esteem or confidence. In that case, strive to increase it to higher measures and appropriately proportional to your potential accomplishments. It should positively impact your behavior, as unhealthy measures will make you proud and overly aggressive toward people around you. So, while trying to develop a healthy level of self-esteem, ensure you don't cause your ego to become overinflated as you shift from its underinflated level.

Importance of Self-Esteem and Confidence in a Teen's Life

For many reasons, having healthy self-esteem and confidence is very important for a teen. You can overcome all the fear and negativity brought about by low self-esteem. High self-esteem and confidence boost your overall performance in all areas of life—academics, relationships, family, and more. You will also conquer all negative interferences in your relationships and overcome all communication difficulties.

Let's look at these in detail. Having self-esteem is important in your life because you:

1. Have no more negative thoughts about yourself

With the right amount of self-esteem, you will no longer have negative thoughts about yourself. Negative thoughts are so damaging to your personality that they can cripple your existence. They are subtle and come in various forms, and you may not realize how harmful they are until the damage is done.

Bad thoughts can make you blame yourself for every wrong that happens. *"If only I had better grades, Mom wouldn't have had heart failure." "If only I hadn't turned off the lights, my roommate wouldn't have slipped and broken his arm." "If only I had agreed to babysit my little brother, my dad wouldn't have lost his job."*

The right amount of self-esteem will help you see how illogical these thoughts are. With the right level of self-esteem, you will be more objective in your thinking and know when to absorb blame and when not to.

Bad thoughts will also make you anticipate the worst outcomes. Thoughts like, *"There's no way I am getting good grades in this subject"* or *"Girls are never going to like me!"* do only one thing — make you feel you can never do well. On the other hand, good self-esteem makes you see your strengths and how well you can perform.

Having good self-esteem will help you overcome thoughts of shame. You will see yourself as likable and interesting. The thoughts that make you doubt others' goodwill result from low self-esteem, and only healthy self-esteem can make you think otherwise.

2. Recognize your strengths and abilities

Good self-esteem will open your eyes to your strengths and abilities. As a teen, this is the time in your life when you begin to get involved in things you never thought you could do. Your parents and teachers will start allowing you to handle bigger responsibilities because they already recognize your strengths and feel they can trust you with certain tasks. Low self-esteem can mar all that and make you wonder, *"What makes these people feel I can even do this, when I can't?"* With good self-esteem, you'll be glad to pick up challenges and see them as opportunities to explore your abilities and showcase your strengths.

3. Shift the spotlight from your failures and dwell on the positive

Good self-esteem helps you stay positive in all situations. Lack of it will only magnify your mistakes to the point where they overshadow your sense of positivity. Let's say you just participated in your school's sports program, where your team came in second for the relay race. Instead of accepting defeat and looking forward to improving next time, you'd rather brood over how you tripped and fell after handing over the baton in the race's second lap! *"I could have done it better,"* you say, not realizing that the fall didn't stop your team from clinching the first runner-up position. Good self-esteem will "cut you some slack" and allow you to smile over whatever you think was a mistake. It'll help you realize that there are no unforgivable mistakes.

4. Expect the best

High self-esteem broadens your horizon and makes you expect the best no matter the circumstance. It gives you an optimistic mindset, which is healthy for your physical, emotional, physiological, and psychological well-being as a teen. With high and healthy self-esteem, you are cheerful and enthusiastic. That will attract more friends to you, as people will feel comfortable being around you because of your positive energy.

5. Don't be afraid of challenges or situations where you feel others could judge you

Do you know someone who's never afraid of challenges or being judged by others? Do you wonder why he's always so comfortable, even when faced with criticism? It's because he has high self-esteem. This would make you not fear being told you messed up because your mind will interpret it as, *"You can do better next time!"* With high self-esteem, you remember you're only a teen and will have many more opportunities to prove your capabilities.

6. Recognize that you deserve to have fun

Life is beautiful. You're young and deserve to have fun. The teenage years are a time to explore the world and be happy. The only thing that can keep you from taking pleasure in your youthfulness is low and underinflated self-esteem. Having high self-esteem is what you need to be you at this point—a teen growing to become independent.

Having confidence is important in your life because you:

1. Overcome shyness

With a higher level of self-confidence, you will overcome shyness. Because you now place a greater value on yourself, you will have the boldness to face your peers and difficult situations. People appreciate bold teens, though not in a negative way. Self-confidence will make you bold in all you do. If you have to answer or ask a question in class, you won't be shy because the focus isn't on you but on the brilliant ideas you have to share with your classmates. Low confidence will attack your personality and ensure you keep your hand down. Self-confidence, however, helps you realize you have a lot of intellect, and those around you should benefit from it. Self-confidence also opens your eyes to your rights as a human to seek knowledge where you lack it.

2. Have no more communication difficulties

Perhaps, you've been having difficulties communicating with your parents, friends, and classmates because you lack self-confidence. Self-confidence will make you more articulate in expressing your thoughts, intentions, and decisions. You will be happy to speak up, not just because you have something to say but also because you are worth listening to.

3. Rise above social anxiety

What makes you feel you're a social misfit is nothing short of low self-confidence. Even as a teen, you have a place in whatever social sphere interests you. Who says you can't run for a position in your student union's government? When you're confident in yourself, social anxiety won't keep you from having your voice heard.

The Benefits of Self-Esteem and Being Confident

The benefits of having self-esteem and confidence include:

1. They bring you happiness

Self-esteem and confidence can make you happy. They help you understand that the first reason to be happy is YOU. You must have heard that "happiness is by choice." It takes a healthy level of self-esteem to be happy with who you are and with those around you.

2. You gain respect

When you exude confidence and high self-esteem, you earn respect from your peers, parents, and teachers. You can't hide self-confidence — it shows in your words and actions. It gives the other person a sense of wanting to respect you and not treat you shabbily. If you wish your friends would treat you respectfully, you must stop being timid and become more confident.

3. You can reject ill-treatment

A good amount of self-esteem and confidence gives you the willpower to reject any abusive treatment meted out to you. Teens sometimes get caught up in abusive relationships that cause pain and confuse them about life. Self-esteem and confidence help you quickly reject such toxicity because you know what's not right for you. You can seek ways to escape such bad relationships only if you are confident that there's help awaiting you outside that toxic circle.

4. You'll become resilient

Teens with low self-esteem quickly bow down when they should be resilient. With self-esteem and confidence, you can persevere and be resilient in navigating challenging circumstances. For instance, you are not likely to drop out of school because you face difficulties with a particular subject or course. You are strong enough to brace up and do all it takes to succeed in your exams and get good grades.

5. You'll practice self-love more often

Self-esteem and confidence will make you love yourself for who you are. This self-love also makes you want to take proper care of yourself physically and emotionally. It's common for teens with low self-esteem to give up on themselves once they face disapproval. But with high self-esteem and confidence, you are careful not to allow disapproval to weigh you down to the point of making you emotionally unstable.

6. *You are a better decision-maker*

Self-esteem and confidence will help you make the right decisions as a teen. You will not give in to wrong choices just because you're trying to please everyone. You can confidently make decisions in your best interest because you put yourself first. Even if it's a family tradition to get a college education at a particular institution, you can boldly decide to study elsewhere if that is best for you and makes you happy. You need self-confidence to make your family understand why you have decided otherwise. You can boldly defend your good decisions when you have self-confidence and high self-esteem.

Finally, we must stop treating ourselves badly. Let's be *our own best friends*. Isn't it funny that we never want to hurt our loved ones, and yet we keep being self-critical without remorse?

The next chapter will discuss common self-esteem issues affecting teens.

CHAPTER 3:
MAIN SELF-ESTEEM ISSUES AFFECTING TEENS

Positive self-esteem is very important for you. This is because you are at the most important stage of your life, a period when your actions and reactions to situations are what shape your personality and prepare you for the future.

But, unfortunately, factors such as your environment, upbringing, negative social interaction, and conflicts begin to tell you a different story about who you are and who you ought to be, and that's how your self-esteem takes a plunge.

Consequently, low self-esteem creates broken, damaged, and abusive adults. This happens because you'll most likely react with bitterness once you sense you're never good enough or pretty enough, or you never appear to fit in with society. This is either borne out of the bitterness you were accorded or a need to disguise your vulnerability. You can easily be taken advantage of or used and abused repeatedly.

A critical analysis of issues affecting teens' self-esteem shows that it is their environment that's mainly responsible for the low self-esteem teenagers experience. The negative impact of an unhealthy environment on your growth and development cannot be overstated. It is evident in the outcome of research involving teens raised in unhealthy environments versus those raised in healthy environments. Potential negative impact is characterized by unsupportive parents, highly critical school authorities, constant conflict in the neighborhood, uncaring mothers, and other factors.

Though it's known that an abusive environment is the underlying factor responsible for low self-esteem among teenagers, it may be difficult to discern a toxic environment if the scenery is beautiful or the people seem very nice and welcoming. In other words, just because an environment appears welcoming or comfortable doesn't mean the underlying social interaction is not toxic.

Issues Affecting Teen's Self-Esteem

If you are one of those who feel less important, less privileged, or like you're not worthy of anything good, take a look at some of these issues to identify and understand how you may have come to have this feeling:

Constant Criticism

When you are constantly criticized in school or at home, negative feelings come with it. Naturally, the reaction of being criticized for everything you do is a feeling of not being good enough or not being able to get anything right.

Even criticism delivered in a positive way can affect your self-esteem if it constantly happens. For instance, if Mr. K. always has to keep a smile on his face as he suggests how you can improve your addition skills, it still means he thinks you are hopeless with your sums. Or if, after a fun session of basketball training, your mother says she's glad you had a good practice even though you are not shooting properly. Despite these positive intentions, it can appear to you that you'll never be able to do anything right.

This can make you:

- Have an identity crisis, which is the main source of low self-esteem
- Have negative and destructive thoughts that bring on consistent pessimism
- Always feel insecure and never want to try something new or take risks
- Lose confidence in yourself

These results are the reasons why you may withdraw and constantly feel the need to be alone. Another effect of constant criticism is when you become manipulative about taking responsibility. Either way, it kills your confidence that you can do certain things and achieve them on your own.

Bad Parenting

Bad parenting is not just about parents who curse, yell, or are overly critical of their kids. Studies have shown that overprotectiveness is a bad parenting strategy that can produce teens who lack self-confidence and exhibit low self-esteem. Bad parenting can also be apparent in super-busy parents who have no time to check out their kid's school work, let alone give praise or correction when needed. It can also show up when parents are too busy to monitor their kids, understand their feelings, or know the type of people they are friends with.

Check to see if your mom or dad does any of these things:

- Doesn't allow you to take responsibility for your actions
- Becomes so protective that they don't let you make your own mistakes, let alone learn from them
- Yells or curses at you for every little mistake. Most times, this type of parent tends to constantly remind you that you are good for nothing.
- Has unrealistic expectations of you just because they demand high standards. This type of parent demands nothing less than perfection — a counterproductive strategy because it'll make you feel less than you're worth.
- Constantly protects you from your emotions. Rather than learn the cause of such emotion, or identify whether it is necessary, they tend to bribe you out of the emotions instead of helping you deal with it.
- Always punishes you instead of disciplining you. When you are being punished, you'll feel like a bad person. But when you are disciplined, you'll realize you made a wrong choice.

Divorce of Parents

Most teens take personal responsibility for the bad relationship between their parents, even when they clearly have nothing to do with it. If you're like that, you sometimes feel as if you could or should have done something to make your parents stay together. That perceived personal responsibility often leads to emotional turmoil.

On the other hand, the divorce process can also lead to your abandonment, a situation where your parents are too busy or emotional to notice a change in your behavior. Your grades may decline, and you may be exhibiting bitterness that's getting you into trouble at school. Most of the time, it feels as if the world is against you.

When you keep making mistake after mistake, your self-esteem worsens. The worst issue is that you have no one to talk to. And if the divorce gets messy or even if your parents have shared custody of you, it becomes easy to interpret that constant shift from one place to another as proof that you don't belong to any place or don't have a refuge to call your own. When it gets overwhelming, your self-esteem takes the fall.

Social Media

To get immunity to the influence of social media, you'd need a maximum dose of a sense of self, a sense of purpose, and self-confidence. Otherwise, social media is one big platform that subtly dictates to you what you should or shouldn't be.

As social media gains popularity, the more you consume certain content that can harm your psychological health. Of course, media has lots of positive effects, but when you get to a point where you cannot do without constantly checking who's saying what or what the latest happening is, you have gotten to a dangerous level of self-reliance on social media.

Studies have suggested that social media greatly affects a teen's self-esteem and can take it to rock bottom. Most content creators are focused on making a living out of social media. Therefore, they put up content showing their perfect, no-mistake side, implying that their world is perfect. While it is good to know that the world can be beautiful, this can become harmful if you start to compare their life with your own.

When you see content portraying that everyone but you is living a beautiful life, has a flawless body type, and maintains a perfect relationship with the perfect person, you can't help but compare their lives against yours and probably come up lacking. It's hard to realize those content creators or influencers are projecting perfection from a delusional world.

Sexual Abuse

Sexual abuse is the worst form of abuse. It's more like a betrayal, a violation of a person's vulnerability. It'll leave any victim broken, damaged, and empty. Regardless of whom the abuse comes from, the effect will be there. However, if you were abused by your parents or a close relative, the wounds are especially deep, and the scars are relics of a difficult childhood. In this instance, you're feeling betrayed by life itself.

The main driver of low self-esteem in a sexually abused person is that they take the blame for being abused. Even in the face of a lot of awareness and sensitization, you aren't convinced it wasn't your fault.

Do any of the following questions haunt you?

- *"Why me?"* This question has no answer, but then you find yourself checking for possible reasons why your abuser chose you. That question can haunt you and lead you into depression. There is no answer to *"Why me?"* because your abuser is a mentally deranged person who does not think before picking his victim.
- *"What did I do to deserve this?"* Here, you wonder if it was your fault that you were abused. You begin to wonder if it was because of how you walked,

dressed, or demonstrated your friendly disposition. This is why most sexually abused people withdraw from social life. They tend to have a very awkward fashion sense because they try not to dress in a way that might attract an abuser.

- *"Could I have stopped my abuser?"* You are often haunted by the thought that you may have contributed to the abuse (especially if it happens more than once). Your abuser understands your vulnerability and takes advantage of you, but through the hurt, you wonder why you couldn't do what you needed to do to stop them.

At the end of the day, you won't find the appropriate answers to these questions. That's because being abused was not a choice you made, and so there's no way you could have responsibility or any answers to these uncertainties. As a result of having these traumatic, unanswered questions in your head, you:

- Lack trust in real friendship. You believe people always want something from you.
- Don't believe there's such a thing as real intimacy
- Are often ashamed. It feels like the world is staring at your nakedness, and you always want to hide away from everyone.
- Can't trust in love, even if you find it

Negative Peers

You'll agree with me that peer pressure can be depressing sometimes. While some kids easily get over it, some find it difficult to escape the influence of negative peers.

The degree of impact from a negative peer depends on the parenting you get back home. It'd be easy to get over it if you had a supportive, available, and attentive parent. On the other hand, peer pressure can remain detrimental when you have parents who are too busy to care for you or are abusive themselves.

Toxic peers manifest their negativity, which can harm your self-esteem, in the following ways:

- *Bullying:* This situation usually targets anyone considered in the minority, such as at a social gathering consisting of rich kids and one other whose parents aren't as well off. Or, in a group of mostly White kids, the Black person can face bullying. The consequence of this unending cycle of bullying is that it negatively affects academic achievement and leads to a devastatingly low level of self-esteem. Feeling unwanted, lacking self-belonging, and experiencing diminished self-confidence can cause suicidal thoughts.

- *Pranking*: While pranks may not be as devastating as bullying, they are self-esteem killers as well. For example, some pranks make the victim the center of a joke, ignoring the fact that they might be going through some difficult situation in their life. It becomes worse when a prank always picks on a particular person, making a joke of them. It is not funny when you are the joke and when this happens constantly.

- *Idolizing Peers*: It's okay to admire someone because they are smart or have a charismatic personality that makes them loving or endearing. But when you start idolizing your peers, you have gone to the extreme of admiration. When you idolize another person, you have successfully put down your sense of self or purpose. You've begun to act like that person, talk like that person, and most likely set yourself up for being bullied by the person. As a result, you will be unable to unleash your inner potential because you will only follow after your idol. Each time you try to do something different from what your idol is doing, you are bound by a subconscious fear. You are bound to be miserable if you are separated from that person.

Also, if you move with the wrong set of people, they could be a bad influence on you. For instance, hanging out with a group that is not interested in taking their academics seriously can gradually affect your grades. And if you consistently get poor grades in school, this can leave you feeling that you are not capable of getting *anything* right.

A negative peer makes risky choices, takes nothing seriously, and uses harmful substances. If you hang out with such people and begin to do what they do, you've set yourself up for self-entrapment, which will eventually affect your self-esteem.

PTSD

Post-Traumatic Stress Disorder (PTSD) can also affect your self-esteem. Trauma affects how you see yourself and your relationship with yourself. Especially when the traumatic event seems as if it should have been avoidable, you start blaming yourself for the turn of events.

One major effect of PTSD is the tendency to expect the worst outcome in every situation, no matter how highly improbable the worst outcome is. This is called catastrophic thinking and is a kind of cognitive distortion caused by a traumatic experience. It is a standard belief system that anticipates only negative outcomes. This kind of belief pattern kills any positivity in you so well that you don't trust yourself to engage in anything good.

The cause of the trauma usually determines the kind of things that raise your self-doubt. For instance, you'll have trouble driving again if you've had an accident. The only thing that'll keep coming to your mind could be, *"I'm bad at driving, and if I try to drive again, I'll have an accident."*

The more you react based on your PTSD, the more you develop coping mechanisms to help you live through your self-denial. It's worse if you've been a victim of multiple traumatic situations; you'll naturally develop a coping mechanism for survival. This is when a person develops an Obsessive Compulsive Disorder (OCD) that makes them doubt themselves to the point that they have to keep repeating actions to ensure perfection, which, according to the voice in their head, prevents the trauma from reoccurring. Meanwhile, their self-esteem has taken a plunge because of their inability to be positive and believe in themselves.

You know your low self-esteem is caused by PTSD if:

- You always feel like you've done something wrong when your parent or authority figure calls you. Whenever anyone calls you abruptly, it feels like there has to be trouble or a problem.

- You feel so insecure that you assume you are the center of a joke. Whenever you see two or more people talking and laughing, you conclude that they are talking about and laughing at you.

- You don't trust love. You feel anyone coming close to you has something they want from you. Even when it becomes evident that they love you genuinely, you wonder why they should, and you sometimes feel they're wasting their time loving you.

- You pay much attention to negativity. For instance, a friend might talk about your appearance and compliment you, but then they point out that your hair needs some adjustment. Immediately, you assume that the other compliments are flattery and that the rough hair perfectly describes how messy your hair or your life is.

Hormonal Imbalance

Actions or reactions to certain situations are influenced by a spike in hormones. This can disrupt your normal behavior and make you react irrationally. Hormonal imbalance can increase the chances of mental health problems in teenagers when it alters the brain's normal functioning.

Low or high levels of testosterone or estrogen can result in depression, brain fogginess, and confusion. They may cause low self-esteem, making you want to withdraw from any social function. Also, if your system is too stressed, it can produce a stress hormone called cortisol, which interrupts your normal ability to cope with stress.

Several factors are responsible for hormonal imbalance in a teenager, including genetics and an unhealthy lifestyle. An unhealthy lifestyle and substance abuse, such as the abuse of alcohol or steroids, are mainly triggered by a hormonal imbalance. Hormonal imbalance can also be caused by medical conditions such as diabetes and pituitary tumors.

If you're having issues with your self-esteem due to hormonal imbalance, you can:

- Exercise regularly.
- Abstain from the use of substances and alcohol.
- Eat healthily. Reduce carbonated drinks and general sugar intake.
- Practice mindful breathing, meditate, and listen to soothing messages or songs.

CHAPTER 4:
THE POWER OF BELIEFS
AND DOUBTS

Imagine standing at the edge of a cliff looking at a beautiful beach below. You want to jump into the water, but you're afraid. You start to doubt yourself and wonder if you can do it. But then, someone comes along and jumps before you do. You see that they're okay, and suddenly you feel more confident. You take a deep breath and jump too. And it's incredible!

Doubts are like that cliff. They can hold you back and make you feel stuck. But if you can find a way to overcome them, you can do amazing things. Sometimes all it takes is a little push or encouragement from someone else. So don't be afraid to ask for help, and don't let your doubts control you. You have the power to overcome them and achieve your goals!

Doubts are normal, but they don't have to hold you back. This chapter will reveal how you can unlock your true potential and achieve great things by facing problems head-on and finding ways to overcome them.

What Are Core Beliefs and Doubts?

Core beliefs and doubts are fundamental concepts that can shape your thoughts, emotions, and behaviors. Understanding your core beliefs and how they influence your life can help you cultivate positive beliefs and overcome negative ones. Now, let's look at these two concepts one after the other.

As the fundamental ideas and values that shape our thoughts, emotions, and behaviors, our core beliefs are our deeply ingrained beliefs about ourselves, others, and the world around us. These beliefs are often formed early in life and are influenced by our experiences, upbringing, culture, and environment.

For example, if you grew up in a family that values hard work and perseverance, you may develop a core belief that success comes through effort and dedication. Alternatively, if you grew up in a family that is more laid back and focuses on enjoying life, you may develop a core belief that happiness is found in relaxation and pleasure.

Core beliefs can be positive or negative, and they significantly impact our mental health, relationships, and overall well-being. Positive core beliefs can help us feel confident, capable, and resilient, while negative core beliefs can lead to anxiety, low self-esteem, and depression.

Doubts are the opposite of core beliefs. They are the thoughts and feelings that contradict or challenge our core beliefs. Doubts can arise from new experiences and information that challenge what we previously believed to be true. They can also arise from internal conflicts or uncertainties about ourselves, others, or the world.

For example, if you believe you are smart but you receive a poor grade on a test, you may experience doubts about your abilities. Or, if you have a core belief that people are generally kind and trustworthy but you experience betrayal from someone close to you, you may experience doubts about the reliability of others.

Doubts can be helpful or harmful, depending on how we respond to them. When we are open to examining our core beliefs and considering alternative perspectives, doubts can help us to grow, learn, and develop new insights. However, when we cling to our core beliefs despite evidence that contradicts them, we foster doubts that can lead to frustration, confusion, and even despair.

So, what can you do with this information? First, knowing your core beliefs and how they may influence your thoughts and behaviors is important. Reflect on your values, attitudes, and assumptions about yourself and your world. Ask yourself what you truly believe and why.

Once you understand your core beliefs better, consider the doubts that arise. When you experience doubts, examine them objectively and consider whether they are based on evidence or assumptions. Be open to learning and growing, even if it means questioning your beliefs.

Core beliefs and doubts are not set in stone. They can change over time as we gain new experiences, knowledge, and insights. Don't be afraid to challenge your own beliefs and explore new perspectives. Doing so can lead to personal growth and a deeper understanding of yourself and the world around you.

Also, by embracing doubts and remaining open to learning and growth, you can develop a more nuanced and insightful understanding of yourself and the world around you.

Core Belief Formation and Development

As a teenager, you are at a stage in life where you are starting to figure out who you are and what you believe in. You'll encounter a lot of different ideas and beliefs from your family, friends, and society. Some of these beliefs will resonate with you and become a part of who you are, while others may not make sense or may feel wrong.

This process of forming and developing core beliefs is a natural and ongoing part of human development, and it's something that will continue throughout your life.

Now let's explore some key factors in core belief formation and development.

Family and Culture

Your family and cultural background are the most significant influences on your core beliefs. The beliefs and values held by your family and cultural group are passed down from generation to generation. They can profoundly shape your view of the world.

For example, if your family values obedience and respect for authority, you may develop a core belief that following the rules and listening to authority figures is essential.

Life Experiences

Your life experiences also play a crucial role in shaping your core beliefs. The things you experience, good and bad, can influence how you see yourself, others, and the world around you.

For example, if you experience a traumatic event, you may develop a core belief that the world is a dangerous place. If you achieve a personal goal, you may develop a core belief that you can achieve anything you want.

Peers and Social Groups

Your peers and social groups can also influence your core beliefs. As a teenager, you're likely to be influenced mostly by your friends and the social groups you belong to.

For example, if your friends value academic achievement, you may develop a core belief that academic success is essential. If your social group values athleticism, you may develop a core belief that being physically fit is necessary.

Media and Technology

In today's world, media and technology influence our beliefs and values. The things we read, watch, and listen to can shape our beliefs and attitudes.

For example, if you pay a lot of attention to media that portrays women as objects, you may develop a core belief that women are inferior. Similarly, if you pay much attention to media promoting environmentalism, you may develop a core belief that protecting the environment is essential.

Core beliefs are not always accurate or rational, but they can become deeply ingrained and difficult to change. This is because they are often based on emotional experiences that leave a lasting impression on your psyche.

Therefore, continued experiences supporting or challenging them can reinforce or change them.

Positive Core Beliefs vs. Negative Core Beliefs

As mentioned earlier, core beliefs can be either positive or negative. Positive core beliefs help you feel good about yourself and others. In contrast, negative core beliefs can make you feel bad about yourself and the world around you.

Positive core beliefs are like rose-tinted glasses that help you see the world more positively. They can help you feel good about yourself, your abilities, and your future. Some examples of positive core beliefs include:

- *I am capable of achieving my goals.*
- *I am worthy of love and respect.*
- *I am valuable and have something to offer others.*
- *Mistakes are opportunities to learn and grow.*
- *My actions have the power to make a positive difference.*

Positive core beliefs can boost your self-esteem and make you more resilient in facing challenges. When you believe in yourself and your abilities, you're more likely to take risks and try new things. You're also more likely to bounce back from setbacks and failures because you have a strong sense of self-worth.

On the other hand, negative core beliefs can be like a dark cloud that hangs over you, making it hard to see the good in yourself and others. Negative core beliefs can lead to feelings of worthlessness, hopelessness, and helplessness. Some examples of negative core beliefs include:

- *I am not good enough.*
- *I am unlovable.*
- *I am a failure.*
- *I can't do anything right.*
- *The world is a dangerous and scary place.*

When you hold negative core beliefs, believing in yourself and your abilities can be challenging. You might feel like you're not good enough or that you'll never be able to achieve your goals. This can lead to feelings of anxiety, depression, and low self-esteem.

The good news is that you can change your core beliefs. Although it takes time and effort, shifting from negative core beliefs to positive ones is possible.

Thoughts and Beliefs to Change

You are going through a period of significant change and growth, both physically and mentally. It's normal to have certain beliefs and thought patterns you've developed over the years. Still, being open to new ideas and perspectives is essential to help you grow into a confident and booming adult.

Let's explore some thoughts and beliefs you may want to change to achieve your goals and live a fulfilling life.

"I can't do it."

One of the most limiting beliefs you can have is that you can't do something. Whether it's a challenging academic subject, a demanding sport, or a new hobby, believing you're incapable of success can hold you back from trying.

Instead, try reframing your thoughts to be more positive and empowering. Tell yourself, "I haven't figured it out yet, but with practice and perseverance, I can do it." This shift in mindset can give you the motivation and confidence to take on new challenges and succeed.

"I don't need to learn this."

As a teenager, you may feel like school is a waste of time and that you don't need to learn certain subjects or skills. However, a well-rounded education is vital for personal and professional development.

Take the time to understand the relevance of what you're learning. Whether it's algebra, history, or a foreign language, every subject has unique benefits and applications. Even if you don't plan to pursue a particular field, learning about it can broaden your knowledge and help you become more informed and curious.

"I'm not good enough."

Many teenagers struggle with feelings of insecurity and low self-esteem. It's easy to compare yourself to others and feel like you're not measuring up, but this negative self-talk can harm your mental health and success.

Instead of focusing on your shortcomings, celebrate your strengths and accomplishments. Set small goals for yourself and celebrate when you achieve them. Surround yourself with people who support and encourage you, and don't be afraid to ask for help when needed.

"I don't care about anyone else."

As a teenager, it's natural to be self-focused and prioritize your needs and desires. However, developing empathy and compassion for others can be essential to growing up.

Take the time to learn about the experiences and perspectives of people who are different from you. Volunteer in your community or get involved in social justice causes. Developing a sense of empathy and understanding can help you build meaningful relationships and make you a more compassionate and influential leader in the future.

"I can't control my emotions."

As a teenager, your emotions can be overwhelming and unpredictable. It's easy to feel like you're at the mercy of your feelings, but you have more control than you might think.

Try to develop a mindfulness practice such as meditation or deep breathing exercises. When you feel overwhelmed, step back and identify your specific emotion. Ask yourself what's causing it and what you can do to address it healthily.

"I'm too busy for self-care."

Finding time for self-care can be challenging between school, extracurricular activities, and social obligations. However, neglecting your physical and emotional health can lead to burnout and other negative consequences.

Make time for activities that help you feel relaxed and rejuvenated, such as reading, exercising, or spending time in nature. Prioritize getting enough sleep, eating nutritious foods, and taking care of your mental health through therapy or other resources. By making self-care a priority, you'll be better equipped.

"I don't need to try because nothing ever changes."

It can be easy to fall into a pattern of complacency and feel like there's no point in trying because nothing changes. But the truth is, change is always possible, and it often starts with one person making a small adjustment. If you want to make a difference in the world, start by changing your own life. This could be something as simple as volunteering in your community, reducing your carbon footprint, or standing up to bullies. Every small action counts; together, we can create a better world.

"I can't do anything about the problems in the world."

It's easy to feel overwhelmed by the problems we see in the world, but it's important to remember that we all have the power to make a difference. Instead of focusing on what you can't do, think about what you *can* do. This might involve educating yourself on the issues that matter to you, speaking out against injustice, or volunteering your time and resources to support organizations that are making a difference. Remember, even small actions can have a significant impact.

"I have to fit in with my peers."

As a teenager, it's natural to want to fit in with your peers and be accepted by your social group. But it's important to remember that you are your own person, and you don't have to conform to the expectations of others. If you feel like you're being pressured to do things that you're uncomfortable with or that go against your values, it is okay to say "no." You'll be much happier in the long run if you stay true to yourself and surround yourself with people who accept you and support you for who you are.

"Girls are inferior to boys."

This is a harmful and outdated belief that has no place in modern society. Girls and boys are equal in every way, and it's important to treat everyone with respect and dignity, regardless of gender. If you believe that girls are inferior, it's important to challenge that belief and educate yourself on how girls and women have contributed to society throughout history. Remember, gender should never be a barrier to success or happiness.

Restructuring Your Core Beliefs

Restructuring your core beliefs is a challenging task, but it's worthwhile. Here are some steps to help you get started:

Identify your core beliefs

The first step in restructuring your core beliefs is to identify what they are. Take some time to reflect on what you believe about yourself, others, and the world around you. Write down your beliefs and be as specific as possible. For example, instead of *"I'm not good enough,"* you might write, *"I'm not good enough to get into my dream college."*

Challenge your core beliefs

Once you've identified your core beliefs, challenging them is crucial. Ask yourself if they are based on facts or assumptions. Are they helping you or holding you back? What evidence do you have to support your belief? Is there evidence to the contrary? For example, if you believe *"I'm not good enough to get into my dream college,"* challenge it by asking yourself if you have evidence to support that belief. Have you talked to admissions counselors? Have you looked at the qualifications of successful applicants? What evidence do you have that suggests that you aren't good enough?

Replace negative beliefs with positive ones

Once you've challenged your negative beliefs, it's time to replace them with positive ones. This doesn't mean that you should be unrealistic or deny your weaknesses. But focus on your strengths and abilities to develop a more balanced and accurate view of yourself. For example, instead of *"I'm not good enough,"* you might replace it with *"I have strengths and weaknesses, but I am capable of success."*

Practice self-compassion

Restructuring your core beliefs can be a challenging and emotional process. It's important to practice self-compassion and be patient with yourself. Remember that your core beliefs were formed early in life and may be deeply ingrained. It may take time and effort to restructure them, but it's worth it.

Overcoming Self-Doubt and Working with Your Beliefs

As a teenager, you're likely experiencing many changes and uncertainty, which can lead to self-doubt. But don't worry. Here are some tips to help you overcome it:

- *Identify your negative self-talk* – Self-doubt often arises from negative self-talk. Take time to identify what you say to yourself when you are doubting yourself. For example, do you tell yourself you're not good, smart, or pretty enough? Once you identify your negative self-talk, you can start to challenge it.

- *Challenge your negative self-talk* – When you hear it, challenge it. For example, if you tell yourself you're not smart enough, remember when you did well in school or learned something new. Challenge your negative self-talk with positive affirmations.
- *Surround yourself with positivity* – Surround yourself with positive people who support and believe in you. This can help counteract the negative self-talk in your head.
- *Set small goals* – Setting small, achievable goals can help you build confidence and self-belief. Celebrate your successes, no matter how small they may seem.
- *Practice self-care* – Taking care of yourself physically and mentally can help boost your confidence and self-belief. Ensure you get enough sleep, eat well, and do things that make you happy.

Remember, overcoming self-doubt takes time and practice, but it's worth it. You can achieve great things, and believing in yourself is the first step.

CHAPTER 5:
OVERCOMING
BARRIERS TO GRIT

Grit is the ability of a person to be consistent and persistent with their life goals and achievement. It entails being passionate enough to withstand whatever pressure or discouragement prevents you from reaching a particular goal. Having grit is about having passion, perseverance, and commitment. Grit is what you need to succeed in life. It is one of the key ingredients of confidence and healthy self-esteem. With grit, going through school or whatever career you choose becomes easier. The more you scale through successfully at a particular endeavor, the more you trust yourself and boost your confidence and self-esteem.

That mental toughness that makes you stand strong in the face of problems or achievements is your grit. It is the most important trait of an achiever—they are resilient and can adapt to whatever circumstances they find themselves in. They have a growth mentality and a positive attitude. For them, there is no limitation because they constantly challenge themselves to do more.

Barriers to grit are limitations that don't allow us to harness our potential. Some of these barriers include ingratitude, low self-esteem, and impatience. This chapter will focus on how to overcome your barriers to grit; you can use your abilities to reach your full potential when you get to that point.

Elements of Grit That Overcome Difficult Challenges

The most important elements of grit are:

1. Passion

People with grit are always passionate about what they do, and this passion is followed by a deep sense of purpose. Once there is clarity about what you want to do or whom you want to become, based on the value system you were brought up with or a belief you developed, it's easy to be passionate about the goal. Passion is that drive that makes you ignore obstacles and limitations to your goals.

2. Perseverance

You cannot describe a person who has grit without mentioning their perseverance. People with grit have a great dose of perseverance borne out of passion and a sense of purpose. Perseverance is when you can hold on to your goal no matter the circumstances; you're not going to just quit. So, it's important to have goals and, when you do, don't assume it's all going to be rosy or that achieving them will be a walk in the park. Be ready to preserve and stay true to your goals.

3. Resilience

Do you know that the "Father Inventor," Thomas Edison, made thousands of prototypes of the incandescent light bulb before finally getting it right? Despite Edison's many failures, one thing was clear — he remained resilient and never allowed his failure to discourage him from pursuing his goals. He believed his failures showed him a different way to get it right. Due to his resilience, we now have some of the most amazing inventions of the 20th century, which include the motion picture, phonograph, and telegraph.

This is what resilience is about — unrelenting capacity in difficult times. It's what propels you to say, *"No matter how many times I fall, I will rise again."* It's a trait you find in optimistic people.

4. Courage

Thinking of courage as the absence of fear automatically disqualifies you from seeing yourself as courageous. Courage is not only when a person does something outstanding; it's about standing up for the right cause when others back out. Courage is taking chances and not giving in when you find yourself in difficult situations. Courage is what the Wright brothers had when they kept failing at their goal of building an airplane yet went on to succeed. Courage is when you can say the truth in the face of intimidation. It is when you are not afraid of being unpopular because of your opinion so you can always do the right thing.

5. Conscientiousness

This is when you thoroughly study what's rational and irrational before taking action, airing an opinion, or choosing a stance. Your courage, passion, and perseverance might be channeled into irrationality if you aren't conscientious as well. At the end of the day, any resultant failure will taunt and mock you. Therefore, you must be diligent and careful, taking calculated steps. Conscientious people don't dive into anything without asking the right questions. In most cases, they tend to be perfectionists because they always want to ensure things are done properly.

To find your grit, there are levels you need to unlock.

We'll be discussing them below:

1. Connect to Your Values and Sense of Purpose

Your values entail who you are and how you interact with your environment. They define your personality, and you'll find them at the base of everything you do. If you are unsure of your values, you can:

Identify Yourself

The best way to identify your values is to honestly answer the questions below:

- What makes you happy the most?
- What activity gets you the most excited? Why?
- What gets you angry the most?
- What is the most important decision you've made? Were you happy about the outcome?
- What would you like to be known for?
- What is most important to you?

Work on Being a Better Version of You

The next step is for you to start working to improve yourself. Work on being the person you want to be remembered as. You can start challenging yourself daily to do one thing that brings you closer to being that person.

What about your purpose?

The benefit behind courage, passion, and perseverance is achieved when you have clarity about why you are pursuing a particular course. Therefore, you need to be clear about your purpose for your existence. Finding your purpose is the inner compass that guides every action you take.

There is a concept known as *Ikigai* in Japan. *Ikigai* means that you should pursue your happiness. To channel your life's pursuit into something you love doing and get rewards for it, you need to:

Have a growth mindset

Each day, work on improving and watch yourself live a fulfilling life. When you have a growth mindset, you'll see challenges as opportunities to become better. It also makes it possible to accept feedback and criticism.

Have a vision statement

This is a short piece that you can use to remind yourself where you are headed in life. A daily reminder of such words keeps you aligned with your vision and your purpose. It makes you more purposeful each day.

Do a pain conversion

Life comes with challenges, roadblocks, and limitations to achieving our goals. Despite this, learn how to turn your pain into purpose. For instance, if you fail your math test and the teacher calls you out in front of the entire class, you feel ridiculed. In this situation, don't give up. Rather, be more determined to prove to everyone, including yourself, that you can learn and excel in math. At this point, you need to be determined to study more or find some friends who are great at the subject. You can even check YouTube to find some math courses to help you learn.

Find your passion

Pay attention to the things that interest you the most. Pay attention to what gets your attention, and before long you are bound to discover your passion. Passion is the bedrock of purpose; you will live a purposeful life as long as you follow your passion.

Love yourself

Loving yourself is important in finding your purpose instead of living someone else's dream. If you constantly practice loving and forgiving yourself when you make mistakes, you get more in tune with who you are and what you want to be. You then develop self-acceptance, self-compassion, and self-care. You can develop everything but selfishness.

2. Coping with Stress

You are one step closer to finding your grit if you learn how to cope with stress, and you can even triumph after trauma. The things happening to you are mostly inevitable or something you have no control over. Consider this when grieving the loss of a loved one or dealing with emotions from a damaged relationship. For some, their parent's divorce is a traumatic event that affects them for the rest of their developmental stages.

One of the ways to find grit is to learn how to cope with stress. Find healthy ways to cope with trauma. It's okay to respond to shocking or devastating news with disbelief, alarm, anger, or numbness depending on the situation. Some experiences are traumatic and may lead to you having nightmares and losing your appetite or your interest in your favorite activities. In some cases, people resort to the use of drugs or other substances. Some even develop PTSD. Therefore, learn to quickly manage and cope with stress at any point in life when you feel you're losing grip.

How to cope with stress

It's okay to grieve over losing someone or something important to you, and it's okay to express your emotions. However, you must learn how to overcome because if you live in that pain or pressure for too long, you might get lost in pain. You have a life to live and a purpose to fulfill, yet dealing with traumatic experiences and getting over them quickly is easier said than done. But then, you can learn to manage the stress by:

- Taking a break from social media. You might need to take a break if you are a content creator. You can let your fans know you need a break, or you can choose to just shut yourself out. Whatever you decide is fine because your mental health is more important than how a fan feels.
- Taking a break from watching news that will affect you. Avoid the TV, or stick to entertainment or other neutral, interesting content.
- Talking about the traumatic experience to a friend or guardian. Talking about your feelings can lead you to self-acceptance of the situation. This helps you forgive yourself if there is a need to, and it also helps you get over the experience.
- Taking care of yourself. Engage in physical exercise. Try activities that interest you, perhaps swimming, football, walking, or skipping. Engaging in physical activity is good for mental health.
- Talking to a counselor if you think you need help in trying to get over an experience you can't deal with on your own.

3. Mindfulness and Gratitude

Mindfulness is a calm state where you ensure all your actions and movements are deliberate. You put your mind into everything you do. To find grit, you need to learn how to be mindful. It starts with practicing mindfulness exercises that center on learning to be focused, determined, and willful.

Practicing mindfulness:

Step 1: Choose a comfortable position you can maintain whenever you want to practice mindfulness. For example, a yoga position or sitting cross-legged.

Step 2: Choose the right time of the day. Note that you must be consistent with the time and duration that you want for your meditation. The early hours of the day are ideal, as practicing mindfulness is a great way to start your day.

Step 3: Start with mindful breathing. Listen as you breathe in and out, and keep your mind blank.

Step 4: Say positive affirmation to yourself.

When you start this practice, note the following:

1. Don't be too hard on yourself. It is quite normal for you to find your mind wandering. Rather than beating yourself up for being unable to get it right, or giving up on yourself altogether, understand

that you're a beginner, and worthy things take time.

2. Develop a sense of self-trust. Believe in yourself — just the act of starting out proves that you're not only willing to do it, but you can do it perfectly. The more you catch your mind wandering away, the better you become at returning your focus.

3. Do not struggle with yourself. The purpose of mindfulness is not for you to strive; instead, you want to understand yourself and appreciate who you are. It would be a mistake to scold yourself each time you find your mind wandering. Your main aim should be to maintain that focus at the same place and time each day.

4. Practice gratitude daily. This helps you place your positivity on a large scale. Think of five new things to be grateful for daily when practicing mindfulness.

5. Some studies suggest that gratitude gives a person a greater sense of purpose. Being grateful is not exactly based on the general good that has happened to you; rather, it's about being grateful for minor things, such as that you woke up in the morning, went through your classes, and got home safely. You can even be grateful for participating in a test, even though you failed or didn't get as high a grade as you expected. Be grateful you have a home to return to.

If you are not okay with being fixated in a particular position, it's okay. It does not mean you can't meditate in another way. You can meditate while listening to music or engaging in a calming activity. You need to apply the basic principle of mindfulness to whatever you do. The goal is to silence whatever is happening around you and focus on your mind.

4. Find Your Cheerleader and Grit Community

It's easier to find grit when you know your cheerleader and can identify with your kind of grit community.

So, the first question is: *Who's your cheerleader?* In this sense, your cheerleader is your motivator. Many young people find it in their parents. However, if you don't find it in either of your parents, you might find it in a person who's always encouraging you, motivating you, and standing by you no matter the circumstances. Cheerleaders are very important because their presence gives meaning to our lives and significantly improves our mental well-being.

When you are with people that inspire or motivate you, there's no way you are left without a purpose or even with little passion for your purpose. Think about that when seeking out your cheerleader. Evaluate their personality, and make sure they are inspiring enough for you. Your cheerleader should be someone who lifts you up, has your back, is not overly critical of you, and will constructively criticize you.

Most times, cheerleaders are found within a grit community — people of like minds who support one another's vision. It might be a group of friends or members of a social or sports club. If you diligently search, you are bound to find one. Otherwise, you can start something interesting that allows you to build a community of like-minded people. Being part of a group gives you a sense of belonging because you are with people who share similarities, visions, and aligned goals.

Being part of a cause can also give you a great sense of purpose. You can join a community of people that provides food for the homeless and needy. You can be part of a community that raises funds to help people fight cancer. You can be part of a group that is trying to provide more technological solutions to make the world a better place.

Joining a cause helps you give back to society. And giving back to society gives you a greater sense of responsibility toward making the world better. Not only that, but you are also bound to find those who'll inspire you the same way your presence in that community inspires others. Ultimately, you are the one who lives with a sense of fulfillment, gratitude, and self-esteem.

CHAPTER 6:
STRATEGIES TO
FAST-TRACK SELF-ESTEEM
AND BOOST CONFIDENCE

How do you feel when you're among your peers? Do you suddenly develop knocking knees when you walk into your classroom? If you find yourself avoiding people and certain situations because you lack confidence and feel you don't belong there, that is about to be a thing of the past because this chapter aims to help you build unlimited confidence and fast-track your self-esteem.

This chapter will discuss practical steps and strategies to improve and accelerate your self-esteem and confidence. The aim is to get you on track in getting ahold of your life, surmounting your challenges, and achieving your goals.

The Step-By-Step Strategies to Fast-track Your Self-Esteem and Boost Your Confidence

1. Make a list of all your strengths

Do you have talents? Are you gifted in any way? Are there things you have an interest in and do them so well it's like second nature to you? I know you do because every young person has something they're interested in. These are your strengths. Please take a moment to think about them and write them all down.

Your list should look like this:

- *"I'm a great football player."*
- *"I'm a smart, proactive, and brilliant kid."*
- *"I'm good at calculus."*
- *"I'm a fast reader."*

The aim is for you to ultimately focus on these strengths. There'll be times when you feel low; on such days, you should read your list out loud and remind yourself of your "strengths." Tell yourself how amazing you are.

2. Learn to face your fears

Fear is the main fuel for a lack of confidence. What are those things that you're afraid of? It would help if you began to face them head-on. You maintain and increase your self-confidence when you face your fears. The next time you're faced with something you've always dreaded, confront it and see how happy and confident you'll become.

See some practical situations below.

- If you're afraid you're not good at art, join a free art exhibition and share some of your paintings.
- If you're afraid of singing because you think your voice isn't good enough, join the school choir.
- If you're afraid of talking to strangers, talk to three people the next time you go to the movies.
- If you think you don't write well, join the writing club at your school.

3. Follow your passion

Follow your passion and do things you enjoy to boost your self-esteem and confidence. Doing this makes you accomplished; you will feel unique when you do those things that make you happy. You may find interest in art, dance, or a sport. Go for it, as that increases your confidence.

4. Show yourself kindness

Be kind to "YOU." You deserve your forgiveness when you "mess up." Stop being hard on yourself—you're not the only one who makes mistakes. Come to think of it, would you be so hard on your best friend? That's the point! See yourself as your "buddy" and show yourself the same kindness and understanding you'd show your buddy. Tell yourself things such as, *"I'm getting better."* Most importantly, learn from the experience and strive to improve next time.

5. Never compare yourself to others

You are unique, different from every other person. So, stop measuring yourself against the successes of other people. When you think some other student is doing well academically, you shouldn't feel bad if your grades are lower than theirs. Or stop comparing yourself with a classmate because he has more friends than you do. He's not the perfect standard for success. You may never know what he's going through; he may have challenges unknown to you and be miserable when others are not around! You will only be unfair to yourself if the classmate becomes your standard for happiness.

Does that mean there's no standard with which you can measure your performance? Of course, there is. But rather than compare yourself with others, you should use your past performance as your yardstick for measuring success. Compare your present performances with your previous ratings and see how well you have improved. It would help if you strived to outperform your previous feats and not the accomplishments of others. Remember that you only see what people want you to see, and you don't know about their shortcomings.

6. Crave new experiences

You only know what you're capable of once you try new things. Your horizon becomes broadened when you crave new experiences. We're not talking about chasing your passions and hobbies here. We're talking about doing things you've never done before. Get a pen and list experiences you'd love to have. It could be climbing a mountain or saying hello to twenty strangers in one day! It may sound like a silly idea, but no, it isn't. You'll find your confidence hitting new heights when you try new things. So, start making that list now!

7. Eat healthily

Your energy levels are at their highest when you eat healthily. You look and feel good when you ensure you eat a balanced diet. Consume more fruits and veggies. Cut down on junk and sweets because they don't give you the nutrients you need to look your best. When you eat healthily, you feel great, and your confidence increases. You should talk with your mom if you need help combining your meals to achieve a proper, balanced diet. Parents are experts in making us eat healthily! A quick tip is to grab a fruit when you need a snack or substitute a glass of fresh juice when you want soda.

8. *Silence negative thoughts with positive self-talk*

Everyone has this voice inside that criticizes them and makes them lose confidence. You hear things such as *"You're not good enough"* inside you. Those are your thoughts, but they're negative ones. You must understand that you have the power to change those thoughts. Replace those demeaning thoughts with positive affirmations. Verbally affirm yourself and watch your self-esteem and confidence rise.

A simple exercise you can do is stand in front of the mirror, look at yourself eyeball-to-eyeball, square your shoulders, and speak positive things to yourself.

Here are examples of words you can say to yourself:

- *"I love myself."*
- *"I believe in myself."*
- *"I am handsome (beautiful)."*
- *"I can succeed in anything I do."*
- *"I am proud of myself."*
- *"I can make good grades."*
- *"I am strong."*
- *"I am confident."*
- *"I am lovable."*

It may seem awkward when you begin this exercise, but continue to do it daily. You will discover that it becomes easier and more enjoyable over time. You will even start to look forward to that part of your day. Also, you mustn't self-talk only in front of the mirror. Feel free to use those words anytime your inner critic starts to speak, irrespective of where you are at the time.

9. Get adequate sleep

Sleep experts suggest that we boost our confidence when we get enough sleep daily. Teens get more sleep than the average adult. While adults require seven hours of uninterrupted sleep every night, you need at least eight to ten hours daily. Remember, your body is still developing, and you're still growing. When you don't get enough sleep, your mind will not be sharp and articulate. It will help if you cut down on the late-night movies that make you sleep late, wake up sleepy, and feel low in the mornings. Develop a sleep routine. Go to bed early to get all the sleep your body deserves. It'll also help if you maintain a regimen of going to bed at the same time daily, which enables you to fall asleep quickly.

10. Gracefully accept commendations

Dad thought you were amazing for fixing the faulty light bulb; that's why he was happy with you. He must have commended your effort too. It's typical for the criticizer within you to dismiss such compliments from others. You should respond with a smile when others say kind words to you. Accept them joyfully. Know that you deserve to get compliments. Don't shy away anymore. Accepting compliments and commendations will boost your self-esteem and confidence.

You can do any of the following the next time you receive a compliment:

- Smile and say, *"Thank you very much"* or *"That's so thoughtful of you."*
- Include that compliment in your self-talk and strength list.
- Respond to the compliment by complimenting the person.

11. Wear what makes you happy

Do you know you can be happy when you look good? That means you should dress in what makes you feel good. Stop allowing current fashion trends to dictate what you wear. Instead, create a wardrobe of outfits that make you happy. Your confidence increases when you look good. And your self-esteem boosts when you wear your favorite fragrance. Try it!

12. Meditate daily

Meditation helps you develop a calm mind that improves your self-esteem and confidence. Meditation makes you think objectively and not judge yourself unfairly. You can meditate at any time, wherever you are. Search online for materials and videos on meditation and start your journey to better self-awareness.

13. See setbacks as opportunities

No matter how painful failure is, you must understand that it's a vital and inevitable part of success. How many times did notable scientists fail before their groundbreaking discoveries?

Thomas Edison had 1,000 failed attempts before creating the first light bulb. Sir James Dyson had 5,126 failed attempts before getting a properly working cyclonic vacuum. Oprah Winfrey got fired from her first TV job before becoming the "Queen" of TV talk shows. The list is endless.

What these notable people did in the face of failure was to see opportunities to get better at what they failed at. They didn't allow the temporary setback to steal their confidence in their abilities. Instead, they made those failed attempts a part of their success stories.

Subsequently, develop the same attitude to boost your self-confidence. See opportunities in failures—opportunities to do better.

Let's examine some practical examples below.

Let's assume you aimed for "A"s in all your subjects or courses and ended up with "B"s and just one "A." Tell yourself, *"If I come this close, then I believe I can get all "A" s next semester."*

Or, if you get rejected from the school sports team because you didn't meet the minimum required performance, rather than give up so soon, do better in the areas you feel set you back and give it another shot.

14. Make a big deal out of your little successes

One thing that opens your eyes to how amazing you truly are is recognizing your every accomplishment, no matter how small you think it is. Little successes are essential for your self-esteem and confidence. So, you fixed the faulty light bulb, and Dad is glad he didn't have to call the electrician. Now, there's a reason Dad is happy. It's worth a lot that you just saved him some time, and he's happy about that. So why shouldn't you pat yourself on the back?

Recognizing that you are good at fixing that faulty bulb is a way to boost your confidence. From now on, don't make light of anything you do well. Being good at any task puts you ahead of many other kids, so take pride in your abilities.

Below are examples of other accomplishments you previously thought didn't matter, but which you should celebrate.

- Sticking to a New Year's resolution
- Getting compliments for a job well done
- Finishing a term paper or project
- Winning an award in school
- Baking a birthday cake
- Taking steps to quit a bad habit

15. Get a support system

There's a need for you to have a support system. Identify positive and supportive people and surround yourself with them. They will help you stay focused on your strengths and best potential. Moments with such persons leave you happy, bright, and optimistic about life. Such positive interactions boost your confidence. Whenever you're feeling sad, talk to them. If they're miles away, then give them a call. They'll help you analyze issues objectively and give you reasons to go on. You will be more confident and focused after such calls. So, what do you do with the rest of the family that aren't so supportive? Learn to ignore their negative talk and remain focused.

16. Smile more often

Smiling makes you feel better and more confident, so smile more often. Smile at others, and most importantly, smile at yourself. When things don't go well, don't frown. Smile instead. When you get a negative report about something, smile. It has a way of easing tension and making the situation appear not so drastic after all.

A helpful exercise you should partake in daily is to smile as soon as you're awake for the day. Starting your day this way makes you more confident to face what it holds.

17. Take more selfies

Young people love to take selfies. Research shows that several selfies can boost your confidence. So, what are you waiting for? Get busy with your phone and reward yourself with high self-esteem as you smile over your different poses. Take it a step further by changing your social media display images often. You're sure to feel better about yourself and get more confident.

18. Exercise regularly

Exercise makes you healthy and is one sure way to care for yourself. When you exercise, your confidence increases, and your self-esteem steps up. You almost feel like you can speak in front of the whole world! Exercise regularly. Make it a habit. Devote at least half an hour to exercise three times a week.

And who says you can't have fun while exercising? If it'll make it more tolerable for you, engage in dance exercises or play a game with a friend. You could also walk in groups or with a close buddy. As long as the activity you're engaging in is exercising your body, your confidence will be affected positively. The good thing about exercising alongside a friend is that they'll help you maintain your exercise routine so you don't begin to slacken after a short while.

19. Learn to be grateful

Be more grateful for the things that are going well, no matter how small they are. Gratitude breeds joy and happiness and lightens your heavy heart. Keep a gratitude journal from now on and update it daily with a few things you are grateful for. In time, you'll be surprised how long your list has become. Read your gratitude list whenever something bothers you, and you'll regain your confidence quickly.

20. Work on your posture

Experts say maintaining a good posture is a quick way to boost your confidence. Good posture sends the messages *"I was born ready!"* and *"I believe in myself."* That's confidence. Stop using poses that depict defeat and low self-esteem. The next time you make a presentation in front of your class, don't slouch. Stand up straight, square your shoulders, and keep your head up. Maintain good eye contact as you speak, and don't stare at the floor the whole time. Make good use of your hands as you explain things. Don't forget to speak up too.

When you sit, use your chair as if you are comfortable and don't sit on the edge as if you're scared. Good posture encourages others to respond to you in an affirmative and friendly way. From now on, be mindful of your posture.

21. *Quit being a perfectionist*

If you still don't believe it, let me repeat, "Nobody is perfect!" Stop being hard on yourself; let down the standards a little. Cut yourself some slack as you would do for others. Don't strive to be perfect; strive to be your best. In trying to be your best, you must allow some room for mistakes occasionally. That way, you maintain and increase your confidence. Remember that no one was born an expert; they all started as rookies. That realization will keep you confident through the different phases of your youthful development.

22. Offer a helping hand

One good way to increase your self-esteem and confidence is to help others in any way possible. The smiles of people you support make you feel good and more confident. The feeling that you can be a positive force or influence on others is good for you.

Below are some ways you can lend a helping hand to others.

- Walk someone's dog during the weekends.
- Sign up as a volunteer in different help groups for kids, the elderly, and others.
- Offer to clean the house for a sick relative.
- Help an injured person with some gardening.
- Help your classmate understand a topic better.

23. Set realistic goals

You have all it takes to achieve your goals. Committing yourself to a cause and trying to achieve it makes you productive, which improves your self-confidence. I know you have several dreams and aspirations as a young person. Clearly list your goals. Next, break your goals into smaller objectives, steps aimed at achieving your main goal. Finally, begin working on one step at a time. In a short while, you will have realized your goal. Working on each step with perseverance increases your confidence in your abilities. As you succeed in each step, you develop higher self-esteem.

You may decide that your goal is to make good grades so your family will be proud of you. Your smaller objective is to study hard for each semester's academic work. Next, you productively engage yourself in attending classes, going to the library, and partaking in reading groups. You follow this up by doing your best on your tests, assignments, and exams. We'll be discussing a step-by-step guide on goal-setting later.

Now, you must believe in yourself every step of the way. Whenever you're discouraged, remember your self-talk, strength list, gratitude list, meditation, and other valuable strategies discussed above. Make attempts to gain back your confidence whenever circumstances around you threaten it. Do all these and watch yourself succeed in achieving your goals. Furthermore, watch yourself walk with squared shoulders and your head held high!

Keep the strategies discussed so far at your fingertips at all times. Practice them consistently, and you'll see your self-esteem and confidence skyrocket.

CHAPTER 7:
SETTING GOALS FOR
A BETTER FUTURE

So far, you've learned much about improving your self-esteem and building self-confidence. The climax of our journey is here, which is to ensure you set goals for a better future.

This chapter will discuss goal-setting; what it entails, why you need goals, and the essential goals you must set to fast-track your self-esteem-building process and boost your self-confidence.

What Are Goals?

A goal is a desire you want to see fulfilled — something you want to achieve. A goal has a timeline within which you're hoping to achieve it. A goal has to do with how you see yourself in the future. If you're hoping to have graduated from school in the future, then that's a goal. You need to sit down and carefully plan what you're hoping to achieve in the future. Goals are carefully thought out and not casually spoken.

A goal points toward the future. You're expecting to have achieved it in the next, let's say, one or two years, to say the least. However, you can break it down into smaller bits, known as objectives, which require a shorter duration.

Goals are usually significant. Sometimes, you may even think you won't be able to achieve your goals, but don't limit yourself. No matter how big a goal is, it's attainable once you're determined to work for it. You can break it into smaller goals and achieve them bit by bit.

However, you must understand that goals are different from objectives. People use the two words interchangeably, but they're not the same thing and don't serve the same purpose. A goal is more comprehensive; it's about what you hope to have in the future. An objective, on the other hand, is a minor step you can take in the short term to actualize your goal.

A goal is not a resolution. Making resolutions is common, especially at the beginning of a new year, but you'd be wrong to see these as your goals. Resolutions are quick decisions you take on the spur of the moment to do something or abstain from doing something. For example, you may resolve to stop watching movies very late at night. A goal is something more persuasive. Goals are not mission statements or slogans that give you a sense of purpose. Goals are definite targets you work toward achieving.

Why Set Goals?

You need to set goals for yourself for several great reasons. You may think that goals are meant only for adults, but that's untrue. We all need goals to make our lives meaningful and purposeful.

Below are reasons why you should set goals for yourself:

Goals help you stay focused

You will become more focused in life when you set goals for yourself. You won't get easily distracted by unimportant things anymore, which is good for your self-esteem and confidence.

Goals help you prioritize your time

You can best manage your time when you have set goals. Without goals, you can be busy the whole day but remain unproductive. When you set goals, you'll know how to give more time to actions geared toward achieving your success. For example, if you dream of winning the chess state championship someday, you will likely attend chess club meetings for more lessons. You'll prioritize practice times over hanging out with friends. You know that each day of practice draws you closer to being a champion.

Goals give you a sense of direction

When you set goals, they help you avoid living life aimlessly and without direction. Being a teen is not an excuse to not have goals. Life isn't all about waking up, being fed, going to school, and having fun with friends. When you live your life that way, you will have a life without direction. Having a dream of what you'd want to be in one, three, or five years makes you relevant, and you live each day trying to fulfill that dream.

Setting goals gives motivation

You are sharper and livelier when you're looking forward to something. Setting goals for yourself motivates you to do your best as you try to achieve them. You're inspired to wake up and face the day because each day draws you closer to actualizing your dreams.

Setting goals helps to increase your confidence

This is quite obvious! Your self-confidence and self-esteem increase when you set goals for yourself. So, if you've been looking to boost your confidence, you have it. You have a sense of self-worth when you look forward to achieving something. Each successful step toward your goal makes you feel good, leaving no room for feeling downcast. With increased confidence, you can easily overcome challenges.

Goals help to increase your productivity

It's a good feeling when you're productive. It's good to know you can do something meaningful with your life. The feeling is so good that it makes you feel confident. That's productivity. When you set goals, this good feeling increases. That's because you'll be busy pursuing a good course. You'll manage your time better, and as you achieve your goals, you will see the result of what you've channeled your time into. You're increasing productivity, and that increases your self-worth.

Goals give you better control of your future

Wouldn't you like to take control of your future? A sense of confidence overwhelms you when you know you are in charge. Setting goals helps you understand what you want in life. That's one of the hallmarks of someone who has high self-esteem. When things make you feel low, you brace up and shake off the bad feelings because you know where you're headed, which gives you the strength to move on and take control of the situation.

Goals improve your competencies

When you set goals and work to fulfill them, you improve your abilities and competencies. As you carry out the activities that move you closer to actualizing your goals, you become a pro at them. Remember, *"Practice makes perfect."* So, if your goal is to be a good dancer, the more you practice your dance moves, the better you get and the better your performance. Whatever your competencies, you can harness them even better when committing yourself to a life-changing goal.

Goals help you measure your progress

If you want to know how much progress you're making, set goals. Setting goals is a way to tell if you're improving and how much you're improving. That's why breaking down your goals into smaller milestones is advisable. As you achieve one step, you look back at where you're coming from and have a reason to pat yourself on the back and continue. As the saying goes, *"You may not be where you're going yet, but you certainly are not where you used to be!"* Obviously, you've made some progress.

Here is a clear example of revisiting your goal of graduating from high school/college with high grades:

Goal: To graduate from high school/college with high grades.

Objective 1: To always take class attendance seriously.

Objective 2: To do my best on all my tests and exams.

Objective 3: To complete each grade/year leading to my graduation.

With the above goal, you've achieved a milestone once you successfully move to the next class, even without graduating yet. Your performance in the exam preceding your new class is a basis for measuring your progress. Your GPA will also suggest how well you're geared up to make your final good grades. You can tell if your progress is satisfactory or if you should put in more work. Your confidence in achieving your overall goal is also increasing. The dream is getting clearer and closer, and you're more resolved to finish. All this is possible because you set a goal to graduate with excellent grades.

Goals You Need to Set

You have learned what goals are and why you should set them. Now it's time to be sure of the goals you need to set.

What aspect of your life would be appropriate for setting goals? As a teen, you'll be most affected by goals concerning your personal growth, health, relationships, and academics. Below are goals you can set.

Personal Growth Goals

- Learn a new skill.

- Write your first story.
- Start a personal journal.
- Learn how to drive and obtain your driver's license.
- Learn how to cook a whole meal by yourself.
- Go camping.

Health Goals

- Learn to manage stress better.
- Get sufficient rest daily.
- Begin a yoga routine.
- Exercise regularly.
- Maintain a cheerful and optimistic attitude.
- Eat more plant-based foods.
- Lose excess pounds and maintain a healthy weight.
- Stop alcohol, tobacco, and illicit drug dependence.

Relationships Goals

- Build stronger bonds with family and friends.
- Make new friends.
- Improve communication with your friends.
- Manage your emotions better.

Academic/Education Goals

- Graduate from high school.

- Start college.
- Complete a driver's education course.
- Start an internship program (preferably in a field you're passionate about).
- Learn to change a flat tire.
- Learn a new language.
- Learn to change a car's oil.
- Learn to jumpstart a car.
- and others...

Concrete Steps to Setting Goals

Now that you know what goals are and why it's important to set them, it's time to do the actual work — set them.

The suggestions above should serve as a guide for setting academic, health, relationship, and personal growth goals. You can also think of other things you want to achieve that are not on the list. But before we set goals, we must ensure that your goals are SMART!

Your Goals Must Be SMART

"SMART" is an acronym for *Specific, Measurable, Attainable, Relevant, and Time-bound.* Your goals have to be all of that for you to achieve them. Let's look at SMART goals in detail.

Specific: Your goal should not be vague or generalized. It should be clear and defined and explainable to yourself or your accountability partner. Research has proven that specific goals are more likely to be achieved than vague and ambiguous ones. To help you be specific in goal setting, ask yourself these questions:

- Who is this goal meant for?
- Why do you want to achieve it?
- What can you do to achieve it?
- When can you achieve it?

If you can conveniently answer these questions, you have a specific goal. If not, work on getting a more specific goal.

Measurable: There must be a way to measure your goal to tell how much progress you're making. That also helps you know how close to or far from achieving your goal you are. As mentioned earlier, breaking your goals into smaller milestones and steps is an excellent way to ensure they're measurable.

Attainable: Your goal must be something that can be achieved even though it is challenging. Don't decide on an impossible mission as a goal.

Relevant: Set goals that are realistic and relevant to your life. A goal should be something that'll add value for you after you've attained it. With goals, we become better and improved versions of ourselves.

Time-bound: You should give yourself a reasonable time to accomplish your goal. Set a start date and a possible deadline. However, be careful not to set unrealistic deadlines. Your time frame for achieving milestones should be commensurate with the nature of your goal. It's most appropriate to set longer deadlines for complex milestones requiring a more extended period so you don't put yourself under too much pressure. Also, give yourself less time to achieve simple steps so you stay active.

Here are steps to goal-setting.

Write your goals down

You have a better chance of achieving your goals when you write them down. Don't just think about your goals, but get a pen and paper and document them. That way, you can see them, and they'll be real to you.

Constantly remind yourself about your goal

Now that you've written down your goal, keep the list where you can easily see it. It will help if you put it in a place you visit several times daily. Constantly read it to remind yourself of your goals. Your bathroom mirror is a good spot. You can also place it on the fridge.

You must be in control

Don't set goals based on things you don't have control over. If you're setting a goal, then you must be in charge. If you're going to be excessively dependent on others to achieve your goal, then you're missing the whole point. You must be realistic and tell yourself the truth. Set goals only when you can be in control. You can ask for help, but be the one in control.

For example, you'll be in control if you set a goal to lose ten pounds within a year. You will set and control all the steps to achieving that goal. You are responsible for what you eat and how and when you exercise. But when your goal is totally dependent on a friend, and you need to wait for him before you can eat a meal or exercise, if he is unavailable, you will relent. This means you aren't in control.

Have a mental picture of the future

To set an achievable goal, you must be able to see a picture of the future in your mind's eye. If you want to lose ten pounds before next year, you should picture what you want to look like by then. That picture will motivate you each day you exercise and eat right. When challenges arise to deter you from going on with the plan, the mental picture propels you to keep going.

You've just started the process when you set goals. What you've done is to identify what you want to achieve. The method of attaining (actualizing) your goals is entirely different. That is the stage where you put in the work.

Know your passions

You require a passion for achieving goals. What are you passionate about? What are the things that inspire you the most? When you're passionate about something, you don't give up on it quickly. It would help if you had that for your goals — they're long-term, and you must be passionate enough to want to hang in there when the going gets tough.

Break goals down into smaller milestones

Significant goals are often long-term, making them seem abstract at first glance. To make your goal more realistic and attainable, break it down into smaller milestones with smaller timeframes. The plan is to actualize one milestone at a time until you fully achieve your main goal.

Be objective

As you take steps to achieve your goal, you may reach a point where nothing or no one else matters. You become so consumed in your new routine that you overlook other matters. It may mean you are neglecting your friends or family, so try to avoid this as much as possible. Do slow down sometimes to look around you. Take note of important things you've neglected for a while and fix that. You're not abandoning your goal; you're just looking at the bigger picture and avoiding burnout.

Create a plan

When you know what you're trying to achieve, you next plan how to achieve it. What's your plan? If you want to lose weight or get good grades, what's your plan? What steps can you take to actualize each milestone until your goal becomes a reality?

Swing into action

Once your plans are clearly spelled out, swing into action. Your goal cannot achieve itself. You must get up and start work on it immediately. You must begin taking the steps you've written down on paper. If you want to lose weight, start your meal plan and exercise. Do *something*. This line of action is likely to change your usual routine. Anticipate this and know that it's all a part of achieving your goal.

Identify possible hindrances

You will face some challenges while trying to achieve your goals. Some things will make the journey seem unattainable. Don't turn a blind eye to them and pretend they don't exist—that's living in denial. Instead, identify problems so you can tackle them. When you spot challenges and do not shy away from them, that makes it easier for you to surmount them. Ask for help if you need it.

Avoid being lonely on this journey

It's easy to feel alone when trying to achieve a goal. To prevent this, pick out a friend or loved one with whom you can share your goal and progress. It's like being accountable to someone, and doing this will help you remain consistent so you can make better and steady progress. You'll also get support and encouragement from this person when you feel discouraged.

Review and adjust

As you forge ahead, it may look as if your goal is unattainable. Rather than give up, review your goals and plans to see what's missing in them. Next, adjust your plans to see if you can better achieve your goal.

And that's all concerning goal-setting! Stay with me as we move to the next chapter, which discusses the need to be kinder to yourself.

CHAPTER 8:
TRANSFORMATIVE EFFECT
OF SELF-COMPASSION

What do you see when you wake up and look in the mirror?

If you see a pathetic person whose face you feel like scratching because they look extremely ugly, then you're self-loathing. If you would rather cover up your appearance even when the sun is hot, especially when you're with a group of people, because you're ashamed of how you look, then you're self-loathing. And it doesn't end with looks. You're self-loathing if you'd starve yourself after an academic result is less than expected. If you'd rather apologize and beat yourself up later for making a simple mistake at your workplace, then you're self-loathing. There are many examples, but one thing underlines them all — inflicting pain or judgment on oneself because of an external issue or mistake is self-loathing.

But first, let's define self-loathing.

What Is Self-Loathing?

Self-loathing is a fickle yet deep-rooted mental condition that can be sparked by minor experiences or large experiences that are beyond your control. What does this mean? A single academic failure can spark feelings of self-loathing, and experiences beyond our control, like a disfigured face from a car crash, can cause self-loathing. You see, self-loathing is one of the essential ingredients of low self-esteem. You don't think you deserve anything good. You believe only bad things should happen to you. Good people look unfortunate when they stand next to you. You think that every failure you meet is what you deserve and that trying to improve is a waste of time. But that's just how self-loathing in a low self-esteemed mind works. But that's all it is—it's all in your head.

It's a very deep sea to fall into, and it doesn't just happen overnight. Yes, self-loathing is an end product of low self-esteem, but even that has its causes, and some of them build up to form the monster in your head that says you deserve nothing good. A traumatic event from the past that caused a significant change in a life trajectory can lead to self-loathing, especially if it affects the person's outward appearance. It could be an accident, a chronic disease that caused body changes, or a disruptive growth in one or two body parts. Self-loathing is often associated with victims of bullying. Most people bullied in high school tend to grow up with searing hate for themselves. The traumatic experience makes them think they are not worthy of being treated with kindness.

When you grow up in a dysfunctional home, especially where one parent is abusive, violent, alcoholic, or a drug addict, you can grow up loathing yourself. Sometimes, less-privileged children grow up loathing themselves as adults, especially if they cannot break the cycle of below-average living when they're grown. So, they indulge themselves in feeling unfairly treated and cheated. They feel unfortunate and undeserving of the world, a feeling that stems from anger and self-pity.

There are several other reasons for self-loathing, but all those instances spark certain emotions that fuel self-loathing. These negative emotions are anger, self-pity, envy, and desperation.

How Lack of Self-Compassion Drives Low Self-Esteem

The walls of self-loathing can be brought down with self-compassion. The lack of self-compassion drives low self-esteem, so to get rid of the latter, you have to eliminate this lack of self-compassion. How can lack of self-compassion drive low self-esteem? The example below will help you understand.

A little boy of twelve years overhears his parents trading words one day but doesn't think much of it since it's something he's used to. That is, until he hears one of them mention "divorce." It is a new term to him, but he doesn't understand the meaning until two months later when he moves out of the house with his mom. Then it dawns on him that his parents have now separated. He notices how his mom now spends more time with her friends, and his father only checks up on him through phone calls. Then he starts to worry about their separation. He remembers words from their quarrels. Although they're sparsely remembered, the words "make time," "show more interest," "it's too much for one to handle," "take a stand," and "be more attentive" begin to form an idea in his head about their reasons for separation. He loosely stitches the clues together and concludes that *he* is the cause of their divorce.

He begins to do everything by himself so that he is out of his mother's way. He feels enraged whenever his grades are bad because he's convinced he's just no good. He starts to see himself as a destroyer, one who ruins everything he lays his hands on. His grades go south, his smile disappears, and his friends slip away. Thirteen years later, he is a dysfunctional adult—one who runs away from crowds, never opposes the views of others because he wants peace, and never looks in the mirror because he's convinced the reflection in it is horrible. He becomes one adult with terribly low self-esteem.

The little boy shifted from angelic to gloomy after he took the first step to self-loathing — blaming himself for something out of his control. When parents separate, it is never the children's fault.

Lack of self-compassion stems from a larger-than-life view of oneself. Like every flawed person out there, you will make mistakes, get sick, fail some courses, and have uncontrollable or unfortunate things happen to you. It's not a curse; it's the way the universe works. Understanding this helps you steer clear of the first step toward self-loathing — self-blame. When you blame yourself for things beyond your control, you're not being compassionate toward yourself, and this contributes to low self-esteem.

This does not mean you shouldn't be accountable to yourself and others around you. When you make mistakes, come clean and accept your faults, but let it end there. After accepting responsibility for your actions, the next step is working toward creating a better future. Nothing positive comes out of dwelling on past mistakes.

Another sign of self-loathing that fuels low self-esteem is unattainable goals. Perfectionism is the killer of joy. You're human and can do much with the resources around you, but this does not mean you shouldn't strive for even better. By all means, aim for the sky, but inch toward your goals one step after another. Maximize your resources as you reach your goals, but take it one step at a time.

People with a victim mentality do not show compassion for themselves. They believe everything is wrong with the world and not themselves. There are two different kinds of people in this category. While one type blames themselves, the other blames the world. Neither of these holds themselves with any value, and they eventually develop low self-esteem. People who blame the world think they're always treated unfairly and never look inward. They are mostly unaware of the blessings around them and instead obsess about the things they can't have, hating the world for this.

It is very easy to slip into this kind of mind space if you give up on taking each day as it comes. Seriously, the trick is taking things easy, each day on its own, and letting go of the past. The happiest people don't have everything at their disposal. Instead, they use every resource they *do* have, understand their limits, are content with all they get, and move toward their goals. They value everything and everyone around them, and above all, they value themselves. They know the power they wield and love themselves for it.

You don't have to have everything within your reach to be happy. A perfectionist will not be satisfied even if they own the most expensive house. People who blame them-selves will not be happy even if they are complimented by the world's most beautiful and important person. Again, the trick is taking things easy, especially when it comes to dealing with yourself. Like everyone out there, you have a breaking point, flaws, and past mistakes. There's nobody on earth who's perfect or has a perfect past. Essentially, what you need is self-compassion.

To be compassionate with oneself is to be understanding of oneself. It is to be understanding of your abilities and weaknesses. The benefits from understanding and lov-ing oneself ultimately lead to better self-esteem. A lack of self-compassion fuels low self-esteem, and it works vice versa. Self-compassion drives good self-esteem.

Benefits of Self-Compassion

What are the benefits of self-compassion?

Better Self-Esteem

Naturally, this is the final outward look of someone who's self-compassionate. They're more at peace with themselves—confident in themselves and all they stand for. They know they're perfect the way they are, with their flaws and all. They know they have a right to speak just as everyone else does. They know their experiences and stories are as valid as anyone else's. They don't delete their past but are at peace with it and can raise their heads up in the crowd.

Quick Recovery from Traumatic Experiences

The essential idea of self-compassion is the ability to understand one's weaknesses. It is the ability to be there for yourself after a bad experience. It is the ability to comfort oneself like a friend after a fall or traumatic experience. Those kind words you say to your friend or family member when they're going through a hard time are the words used in self-compassion as well. It doesn't sound like self-pity. In self-pity, one blames everyone but themselves. Self-compassion is seeing one's faults even as you comfort yourself. It is actively fighting between the walls of self-blame and self-pity. In that sense, self-compassionate people will naturally bounce back to a more positive state of mind than others after a traumatic experience because they understand themselves, which strengthens them.

Better at Handling Anxiety, Stress, and Fatigue

In the face of anxiety, stress, and fatigue, we react irrationally, which is understandable. When you're anxious, you'll feel like your mind and body are tired, but you don't get a break because life's a constantly rolling stone. It's so crazy that you want to drop into a deep sleep for a few days and disappear from the world and all the activities screaming around you. These kinds of dire situations are better handled with self-compassion. Instead of getting grumpy due to anxiety, use self-compassion to be at peace knowing you'll do your best every chance you get and leave it at that. You're more honest with yourself and your body. You know how much you can take and when it's too much to handle. You wouldn't force an overwhelmed friend to take on more workload than they can handle, and you wouldn't force yourself to take on more workload than you can handle. This way, you take care of your mind, and it gets stronger.

Positive Personal Growth

The kind of growth that comes with self-compassion is immeasurable. When you're at peace with yourself and understand yourself, you know your weaknesses and actively work on them, leading to much growth. Self-compassionate people are widely open-minded and objective. They can easily put themselves in other people's shoes and understand different points of view. They know everyone has flaws, and they don't judge people based on their failures because they know better. In fact, they do unto others the way they want others to do unto them. They put themselves first in tough situations and know how to bounce back after a fall. A fall is never permanent for them. This mindset leads to a lot of growth; a lot of positive personal growth.

Stable Relationships

Because they don't judge or over-criticize themselves, self-compassionate people are not locked up in a single-dimensional world. This helps with relationships a lot. Self-compassionate people are the best team players. They are good accountability partners and emotionally reliable cohorts. They are understanding of flaws and yet committed to change and growth. They see and understand your weaknesses and yet are faithful in helping you overcome these weaknesses and flaws. They don't harbor or tend to negative emotions, which encourages a peaceful relationship free of toxic emotions and reactions that lead to breakups. They are not the best partners but actual humans, who see the humanity in others and themselves.

How to Cultivate Self-Compassion

Getting to a healthier mind space with self-compassion is possible, but it takes work. Most times, therapy sessions can be a stepping stone to reaching that peaceful mind space. However, when the therapy ends, what next? Do you jump back to your old self? Do you resume old habits? The answer is "no" because doing that makes this a vicious cycle. Cultivating habits that build self-compassion is a better ladder to climb to a stronger mind than running a vicious cycle of toxicity and therapy sessions. The list of habits that amount to self-compassion isn't comprehensive. It is not a definite manual but stepping stones in the right direction, approved by research.

Positive Vocabulary Vs. Negative Vocabulary

The first reaction to failure or mistakes shouldn't be name-calling or blaming. When a friend is going through a hard time, you want to alleviate their pain, so you say kind words to them. Why can't you do the same for yourself? Like your friend, you're human and bound to make mistakes. So, when you're in an unfavorable situation, say kind things to yourself. Watch your vocabulary when you criticize and evaluate yourself. Sentences like *I'm useless, it's all my fault, I'm stupid, I'm an idiot, I'm so dumb, I'm so bad,* and so on should be cleansed from your dictionary. Instead, open your mind to accept that you made a mistake. Remind yourself that you will do better next time and that you did your best for now.

Daily Emotional Evaluation and Journaling

You can use journaling to keep track of your emotions. Therapists usually give out journal workbooks that help clients evaluate their emotions and control their mental states. This is also a good method for achieving self-compassion. Writing down emotions and positively addressing them is a big step toward becoming self-compassionate. When you feel a negative emotion, write it down and address it. Why do you feel that emotion? What event sparked it? Address the event. What happened then? What went wrong? Why did things go wrong? This is a step-by-step method of understanding our emotions and putting them in their right place. Should you feel sad? Even when you should feel sad, ask yourself, *For how long?*

Comfort First, Blame Later or Never

It's easier to blame people and ourselves than to say comforting things in heated situations. However, self-compassion involves saying comforting things to yourself when you're faced with failures or traumatic experiences. This means that you tell yourself kind words after making a terrible mistake. Now, telling yourself kind words is different from making excuses for yourself. For example, say you fail to score at least 70% on an exam in college and are held back for one more year. It's easy to say you didn't work hard enough to get that score and call yourself a dummy, but this isn't the first thing to do in such a situation. The first thing to do is remind yourself that you did your best, as you would tell a friend in the same situation. After this, you review the questions, look for parts you found difficult, and work on them. In the end, you don't end up blaming yourself or anybody at all. Instead, you look for solutions instead of blaming yourself or beating yourself up.

Be Thankful

The happiest people are the thankful ones. Being grateful for the tiniest thing brings a lot of peace to mind. You feel lighter and easily see the positive sides of situations. Writing down things you're thankful for at the end of each day can help you be more compassionate toward yourself. When you're faced with difficult situations, instead of blaming yourself, immediately think of things that went right and be grateful for them. This positive outlook gives you a healthy mind to sort through your emotions and objectively judge a situation. Ultimately, you're grateful for your strengths and more understanding of your weaknesses.

Give What You Can Receive

The watchwords for self-compassion are, *"Can I take this?" "Will I like this?" "Do I want to hear this?"* When you comfort yourself, you're telling yourself what you would say to a friend having a hard time. So, when someone makes a mistake, fails, or is a victim of something beyond their control, ask yourself this anytime something mean comes to your mind about them: "If I were in their shoes, would I like this? Would I want to hear something like this at this time?"

A lot of people don't filter their words before they talk. They say whatever comes to mind and are less concerned about how others feel. It can be the same in dealing with ourselves. Sometimes we don't think through what we say to ourselves when we're having a hard time. So, when you ask yourself those three questions before speaking to others, you'll apply the same to your situation. Now you're on your way to becoming a self-compassionate person, and one of the happiest people in the world.

Finally, self-compassion is the salt of great self-esteem. Be kind to yourself because you're beautiful and human, after all. Take each day as it comes, and stay healthy. Put your best effort forward, and stay kind.

CHAPTER 9:
EMBRACING SELF-LOVE

Do any of the following sentences sound like you?

Why don't people love me? Why does everyone seem to hate me and not want me around? What can I do to make people love me?

No doubt, loving yourself can be difficult, especially when you see things about your appearance that you don't like. However, do you know that you're doing yourself a great good by loving yourself? You'll be amazed at the results you'll see when you embrace self-love.

Unfortunately, for many reasons, people choose to care more about the perceptions of others, which makes them act in awful ways toward themselves. When they should love themselves, they choose to subject themselves to their dark inner critic, which has nothing good to feed them. While it can be easy to dwell on your *perceived* inadequacies, have you ever considered yourself and your feelings?

Well, regardless of your reason for lacking self-love, this chapter will focus on why you should start treating yourself right, why you should give yourself the same amount of love you give others, and how you can start caring for yourself.

Self-love isn't selfish. By loving yourself, you tend to show others that you're valuable and how you ought to be treated.

What Is Self-Love?

You can't talk about self-love without first knowing what it means. Self-love is the appreciation you have for yourself. It means loving yourself for who you are. Self-love stems from taking care of yourself and your needs and putting yourself before anyone else.

When you have self-love, you won't sacrifice your happiness for that of others. That is not to say you are heartless, but you won't make yourself unhappy just so that others will be pleased. Self-love means taking actions and steps to support your physical, emotional, and mental well-being.

Self-love also means loving yourself to the point of not settling for less. You avoid accepting situations just so you don't miss out. You are patient enough to pursue what you're entitled to.

For a better understanding of the concept of self-love, I will be introducing you to an imaginary friend, Julie.

Imagine you have been friends with Julie since childhood and have shared many memorable moments with her. Julie's such a sweet girl, just like the rest of her family, which has been close with your family forever. Out of childhood innocence, you and Julie promised to be together forever, a decision you both made in the presence of your families.

Years have passed, and you and Julie have grown into two admirable teens, each pursuing their dreams to be someone great in life. A lot has changed over the years. Your perception of life has changed, and neither of you think as you used to years back. You have become aware of yourselves and now have a different view about what you want in a love relationship. Somehow, your relationship with Julie doesn't cut it for you anymore. Her life view differs from yours, and she sometimes laughs when she remembers the innocent decision you both made as kids.

You have told your families that you two can't be more than just friends and that you've both found love with other people. But your families feel disappointed that your new way of thinking will strain the bonds in both families.

The question now is, what do you do? Are you willing to risk your happiness to please your family? Do you feel you've let down those who love you so much? As we look deeper into the subject of self-love, you'll get a better understanding of how to handle this situation.

Why Is Self-Love Important?

Self-love is essential to building and maintaining a healthy relationship with yourself and others. When you have self-love, you can take care of your needs better. You'll be better disposed to make the right decisions when you consider your needs. Self-love also strengthens you to avoid toxic relationships and maintain functional ones.

You can pick up destructive behaviors and habits when you lack self-love. Lack of self-love resigns you to an unhealthy lifestyle that can lead to dysfunctional relationships and physical and emotional problems.

What does self-love mean to you as a teen?

We all have different ways we take care of ourselves. That implies that self-love means different things to each of us. You must therefore figure out what self-love means to you as a teen. That is necessary for your mental health and can determine your self-confidence and self-esteem.

Recognizing your values

Self-love entails recognizing your values and committing yourself to live by them. What are your values? Are you humane, kind, compassionate, and forgiving? These are all ways you can relate to people and affect their lives.

Nurturing relationships

How do you see your relationship with others? Do you nurture your relationship with your family and friends? If you do, then you have self-love. You also need to clearly define and establish healthy boundaries in your relationships. When you nurture your relationships with others, you will be interested in helping them, using your potential.

Being content with your self-discovery

Self-love is not an assurance that everyone will always be happy with you or your confidence. When you know your self-worth, you'll discover it may not go well with some people. You may lose some friends too. However, you don't have to worry if anyone leaves your life due to your self-discovery. It indicates that they benefited from your lack of self-confidence while it lasted. It may be a good thing if they're gone for good.

Self-care

You practice self-care when you have self-love. You take the following actions of self-care because you have self-love:

- You take breaks to rest from your work at intervals. Be it your schoolwork or a part-time job you picked up, you see the need not to overwork yourself. That is good for your physical and mental health.

- You listen to your body. You don't do anything that'll jeopardize your health. You don't indulge in habits that'll harm your body, such as substance abuse and excessive alcohol. You also don't put yourself under undue stress, as that is not good for your body either.

- You're not glued to your phone all day, as most young people do these days. You know the importance of occasionally ditching the phone to connect with real people. You can also do more creative things with your time rather than spend all day on social media.

- You want to eat healthy meals and drink lots of water, which is good for your body. However, you may still try out your favorite foods sometimes.

The key to self-love is balancing self-care and responding to other people's needs. If you neglect the needs of your family and friends and become ignorant of their interests, your level of self-love is questionable.

One of the ways to measure self-love is to know how healthy and functional your relationship with others is. There's no way you'll be happy knowing that you can't build successful relationships. That realization breeds dissatisfaction within you, lowering your self-respect and self-love.

What Self-Love Isn't

The topic of self-love is complete only if you learn what self-love is *not*. To be clear, self-love is not any of the following:

1. Self-love Isn't Selfish

It's dangerous to think you're practicing self-love whenever you satisfy your needs irrespective of what anyone thinks. That's not self-love but selfishness. While meeting your needs is not wrong, it should not be at the expense of others' happiness. Such behavior shows a lack of self-love.

2. Self-love Isn't Deceitful

A situation where you deceive or exploit others to meet your needs should never be considered self-love. Making other people suffer a loss so you can gain your desires is wrong and shows you lack self-worth, self-love, and self-confidence.

3. Self-love Isn't Insensitive

If you have self-love, you'll be empathetic toward others. You'll be willing to help rather than feel untouched by the plight of others. It would be best to learn to put yourself in other people's shoes to see their plight clearly. Showing empathy helps you understand others better. That way you can decide to be of help to them.

4. Self-love Isn't a Day Affair

Self-love is a journey you will be on for the rest of your life. You don't feel self-love one day and think it'll last forever. You have to continue loving yourself and being nice to yourself. Many days you will feel confident that everything is going well for you. There will also be days when your energy feels depleted, and your mood is low.

You must remain committed to returning to your high level of self-worth so you can continue to love yourself.

5. Self-love Isn't Dangerous

Self-love is not dangerous. It does not cause any harm to others. Even though genuine self-love will place your needs above those of others, it does not deliberately set out to harm others.

6. Self-love Isn't Excessively Egoistic

It's not self-love to seek your interest while disregarding the interests of others. Refrain from pursuing your interests to the point that the concerns of others are negatively affected.

7. Self-Love Isn't Over-Dependence on External Validation

Self-love is not waiting for the approval of others before you feel good. While you're not uncaring about what people say, you don't depend on people's opinions as the measure of being happy with yourself.

8. Self-Love Isn't Over-Dependence on Social Standards

Don't allow what everybody thinks is right to dictate how happy you should be. That's not self-love. You must love yourself irrespective of what is trending out there. You mustn't start drinking because everyone thinks teenagers should have a few drinks. You must be confident to decide on and do what's best for you. Your self-image should never be a result of a justification of social standards.

9. Self-love Isn't Overly Compensating

Self-love is not having to work too hard to compensate for lost ground as a result of something you may have been lacking in your life. For instance, you may not have been eating right for years, and this may have caused you to accumulate excess weight that you now need to shed. You also know you must take care of your health as part of self-care. You don't have to starve your body of vital nutrients because you want to make up for the years you didn't eat right. Losing excess weight is a gradual process that's not intended to harm you.

How to Be Intentional with Self-Love

You have to practice self-love intentionally. When you have self-love, you do the following:

1. You're nice to yourself

You must treat yourself with love, patience, compassion, and kindness. It feels right to treat others nicely, so why not you? You deserve as much love as you show to others, so be nice to yourself.

2. You talk about and to yourself with love

Much of the time, you talk about others with so much courtesy and politeness. It's high time you do the same for yourself. If you must talk about yourself, do it with love because you are valuable. And when you speak to yourself (during your self-talk sessions or at other times), do it with love.

3. You put yourself first

You have to be physically and emotionally stable to be capable of helping others. It would help if you considered your well-being first, before that of others. However, you must carefully draw the line between self-love and selfishness.

4. You are more mindful

Be cautious of your thoughts, feelings, and wants. Don't accommodate negative thoughts that'll dampen your mood. Be careful how you make yourself feel. Don't entertain any air that'll reduce your confidence. Be careful about what you desire. Ensure it's in your best interest and not born out of selfishness.

5. You forgive yourself

Yes, you've done something you're not proud of, making you feel ashamed and humiliated. You've spent the last two months beating yourself up over that mistake. Well, it's time to let it go! It's time to forgive yourself and move on. You can't undo what you did wrong, nor can you change the past. But guess what? You can influence the future. So rather than continue to wallow in regrets, consider the incident an opportunity to learn and believe you can handle the situation better next time. You know you'd gladly forgive someone else for their imperfection, so you must extend that same forgiveness to yourself.

6. You focus on your needs rather than your wants

You don't always have to do or get what you want. Avoid spur-of-the-moment desires; focus instead on what you need. Unguarded wants can make you develop behavioral tendencies that can reduce your self-love, keep you stuck in the past, or get you into trouble.

7. You cultivate healthy habits

Start doing things that will benefit you and then make habits out of them. Eat right, exercise, and practice self-care. Don't do these things just because you "have to" or to "get them done." Do them because you love and care about *you*.

8. You go easy on yourself

The idea that you have to be perfect is false. The perfect lives, figures, and achievements you see all over the media aren't what they are on the surface. Most times, people are only doing their best to hide their imperfections. So, never feel bad that you can't measure up because you're not even supposed to strive for what you see in the first place. Love your biceps the way they are. Exercise because it's one of the ways you can take care of your body and live healthily, not because you must measure up to some "perfect figure" you see on TV. Learn to be happy with yourself, knowing you're trying your best to harness your potential. You are unique in your own way.

9. You practice good self-care

A lot has been said about self-care. Practice it by indulging in healthy activities daily. These include adequate sleep, sufficient exercise, wholesome eating, and healthy relationships.

10. You enjoy every moment

It would help if you deliberately enjoyed every moment of your day. Stop searching for a better time and maximize what is available now. Open your eyes and mind to see how lucky you are to be alive at "this moment."

11. You practice daily gratitude

You show that you have self-love by being grateful daily. Be thankful that you are a functional being who can breathe, walk, talk, etc. It would be nice if you started a blog, social media page, or journal in which you can document all the things you're grateful for. Research suggests that showing gratitude helps you develop positive emotions, improving your general health.

12. You realize you can't control everything

You put so much pressure on yourself and feel inadequate sometimes because you think you can control everything. You feel unhappy when your expectations are unmet, and this affects your self-love. You must realize you can't control everything, and it's okay to accept that. You can control only those things you can change. You can't successfully influence how others act or the decisions they make. Rather than try to control everything, channel your energy into how you respond to situations. Please do your best and leave things to play out by themselves. Resolve to be happy whatever the outcome.

Remember the case study about you and Julie? Wonder why both you and Julie grew up to be different people than you were as kids? You couldn't control your feelings for her over the years, just like she couldn't control yours. Though your families are having a hard time coming to terms with that, the fact remains that they can't control how you feel about each other. That's a great lesson you must always remember.

13. *You remain true to yourself*

Never turn a blind eye to how you feel. Be honest with yourself. Admit how you honestly think about things rather than mask your feelings. That way, you can shut out negative emotions and allow in only the positive ones. You can't get rid of something unhealthy if you don't accept that it's bad for you. If you're on a weight loss journey, you'll continue to struggle if you don't tell yourself the truth — that certain foods and habits are bad for your health. The pleasure you derive from them may make you want to overlook this fact most of the time, but you'll show yourself love when you accept that those things don't mean enough to you, so you might as well do away with them.

The same applies to unhealthy relationships that hurt your self-worth. You must be honest about how those interactions make you feel before you can have the willpower to cut them off.

14. You set boundaries

For you to love yourself, you must focus on yourself. How you spend your time matters. Get rid of all the time-wasting activities that don't add value to your life. Instead, positively invest your time in life-building activities. Don't feel guilty if you have to say "NO" to people with whom you enjoyed those time-wasting activities. It doesn't make you a bad person; it only makes you wise in personal time management.

15. You have someone with whom you can unwind

A vital part of self-love is creating friendships that improve your self-worth. Having a special friend with whom you can share your feelings unhindered would be nice. Discuss how your day went with them and practically unwind to relieve stress. When you can share your day with someone, it makes you happy, and you can love yourself better. Intimate friendships, be they platonic or otherwise, act as valuable support to your emotional and mental well-being.

16. You reduce your stress

Figure out ways to reduce stress. Doing so will help you prevent high blood pressure and depression. You can relieve stress by following a daily routine to rest or nap at certain times. You can also listen to music, relax with friends, or walk.

17. You declutter your social space

It's time to do some cleanup on all your social media handles. Unfollow or block off all haters and bullies in your space. They all have only one thing to offer—"negative vibes." That's the last thing you want to receive from so-called "online friends" in your journey to self-love. You should receive only positive and valuable information from your social media space.

Do You Love Yourself Enough?

In light of all that has been discussed about self-love, you must examine yourself and ask, *"Do I love myself enough?"* Carefully review everything self-love should be and examine yourself to see if you've been practicing these suggestions. It would help if you asked yourself more questions such as:

- "Do I recognize my values?"
- "Am I nurturing valuable relationships?"
- "Am I content with my self-worth regardless of who's displeased?"
- "Am I practicing self-care?"

Also, look inward to see if there are any traces of attributes that falsely define self-love. Are you selfish, insensitive, deceitful, or self-centered? Where do you seek validation? Is it from within you or from unrealistic social standards?

In learning whether you love yourself enough or not, you must be true to yourself. You must answer each question objectively and not be afraid to admit that you haven't loved yourself enough. As discussed earlier, being true to yourself is one way to love yourself. It means you love yourself enough to realize you're not treating yourself nicely and want to change.

After being honest about your state of self-love, take vital steps to show yourself the love you deserve. Practice the steps to be intentional with self-love and note your progress. Remember that self-love is about taking action to improve who you are. You must realize that it's going to take a lot of work. You must, however, be committed to loving yourself and don't give up.

CHAPTER 10:
MOVING FORWARD

After learning the fundamental truths about self-esteem and self-confidence, it's time to move forward!

Moving forward means you're ready to solidify everything you've learned from this book and start living the best version of yourself. This chapter will focus entirely on sustenance and actionable steps to maintain high self-confidence and self-esteem. So far, we've discussed increasing your self-esteem and developing confidence. But what comes next after developing these? We'll move forward and ensure everything you've learned is retained.

This chapter will focus on sustenance and the steps to maintaining high self-esteem and self-confidence.

Let's get started!

Strategies to Sustain Self-Esteem

Here are strategies you can use to sustain self-esteem.

Identify conditions and situations that are troubling to you

You must first identify the uncomfortable situations and circumstances that make you feel uneasy enough to lose your self-esteem. You know the events we refer to and how you sometimes feel compelled to attend them. Such events or situations should serve as a good opportunity to demonstrate how confident and self-assured you are around them.

To sustain everything you've learned about building sturdy self-esteem and developing self-confidence, you must find and understand what triggers you to feel less confident.

If you don't find the conditions that trigger you or make you feel uncomfortable, you won't be able to avoid them. So, carefully consider them; think about the people you know and how they affect you. Do they affect you positively, or do they make you lose your confidence and become intimidated?

Your trigger could be anything, such as hanging out with friends and neighbors, a family function, going in to take a test, or even your classroom teacher. Whatever the situation, don't encourage it to trigger you to feel less confident. Excuse yourself from the environment when it becomes too toxic for you, and consider yourself and the safety of your mental health before any form of friendship.

Be aware of your thoughts and beliefs

If the first step is to identify your troubling conditions, the next is to be conscious and aware of your personal belief system. Imagine yourself as a goalkeeper. The moment you lose your self-confidence, balls will start slipping from you easily. Every goalkeeper maintains high confidence and stays true to their thoughts and belief system to withstand the pressure of their opponents and the force of the ball.

Your sense of judgment is guided by your beliefs; it will determine whether you are on the right track or not. Acting differently from your thoughts is impossible because you are merely your belief system in physical form. Consider an idea based on how valuable it will be to you rather than just because someone else has suggested it.

If your thoughts and beliefs do not align with the positive path you want to take in building self-confidence, you will always struggle with low self-esteem. Let go of any belief systems you may have been exposed to when you were younger and replace them with words, ideas, and concepts that will elevate your mind.

Challenge every negative thought

Don't let any negative thoughts settle in your mind; challenge them and purge them. Negative thoughts will always thrive when you allow them to, which means you'll be full of doubt and held back by such thoughts. If something conflicts with your beliefs, thoughts, and ideas for the future, don't be afraid to change things by making some adjustments.

Although it is good not to doubt yourself, always double-check your thoughts and ask yourself if you're on the right track because your initial thoughts may not always be accurate. Ask yourself, *"Are my thoughts rational? Do the solutions I propose for my issues help me improve my self-esteem, or do they serve to undermine it?"*

Pay attention to your thought patterns as well. A frightening thought is often the result of anxiety and restlessness. When you are afraid, you lose confidence, and your self-esteem suffers. Negative thoughts also cause you to minimize your accomplishments, which is a sign of low self-esteem.

You must examine your thoughts daily to maintain your positive self-esteem and self-confidence. Take a cool shower to wash away the negatives and welcome possibilities into your life. You will no longer undervalue yourself; you will no longer jump to negative conclusions but maintain a positive attitude.

Watch the company you keep and be mindful

Now you know that your beliefs, thoughts, perceptions, and ideas can solidify or shatter your desire to build sturdy self-esteem and self-confidence. However, you might not know that those ideas and thoughts are made real in your head when you allow people to influence you. We are always surrounded by people who influence our decisions daily; therefore, let's be mindful of those who surround and influence us when we want to build solid self-esteem and self-confidence.

Ask yourself, *"Who are the people surrounding me? Who are the people I listen to regularly? Who are my friends? Who are the people I am comfortable sharing dreams and aspirations with daily?"* When you answer these questions, you can recognize the differences between the people in your circle. People in your social and family circle should be supportive and encouraging with positive words rather than those who will undermine your self-esteem.

So, once more, pay attention to those who surround you, and don't be afraid to cut ties with those who aren't adding value to your life. Also, surround yourself with people with great self-esteem and who are highly confident in themselves so that they can help raise you to your desired level.

If the people surrounding you are not contributing to your growth or aiding your dreams, consider limiting the time you spend with them.

How to Regain Control over Your Life

Some of the most important things I learned about regaining control over one's life as a teenager are rediscovering things that make you tick, learning how important it is to care for yourself, and then spending time with your loved ones and the things you love. Here are some powerful tips to help you regain control of your life.

1. Be strict with your "me" time

No matter how hard you work, study, or dedicate yourself to helping others, always set aside time dedicated to only yourself. Your "me" time is a way for you to recharge and get all the boost needed to continue your regular routine filled with energy and enthusiasm.

2. Don't be afraid to go beyond convention

Many people would have thought Bill Gates was crazy when he started his dream in a garage. They didn't know he was busy building his dream and making it come true. He wasn't afraid to break the conventional rules, he wasn't nervous, and no, he didn't need anyone's validation to pursue his dream. He pursued a path meant for him, and he succeeded.

3. Identify internal vs. external motivations

Saying, *"My life is out of control,"* can make you feel like you are just riding along and going somewhere you never really wanted to go. Who is in control of the wheel — you or someone else?

Distinguishing between your internal drives and balancing them with outside influences can help you get back on track and regain full control of your life.

The most powerful driving force is when you are motivated from within. I'm referring to those deepest desires that give you a sense of passion and direction. These dreams, desires, and aspirations are personal to you because they are decided by your personal values and objectives.

External motivators are those that come from outside of yourself. They speak of the objectives and standards established by your family, spouse, friends, or community. External motivators can also refer to societal standards you feel obligated to meet.

Our internal motivations and external motivators may occasionally clash. Your parents want you to finish your master's degree and take over the family business even though you want to quit school and travel the world. You have a family supporting and pushing you from one end, while at the other end, you want to leave your job to pursue your passion.

Regaining control of your life does not mean ignoring all outside motivators. Finding a balance that accommodates both is great if that's attainable. It's not you being selfish. It's an essential balance that lets you stay happy.

To explore further and learn more about what motivates you, you must nurture your relationship with yourself. Learn to set boundaries and find the right balance so you can concentrate on the things that truly make you happy. You can only be there for others selflessly when you are living your purpose.

4. Know when to say "no"

Are you the type that spends most of your time saying "yes" to the request of everyone around? Perhaps you are leading a club, chairing a board, and joining an organization. You are doing all these because you can't say "no" when asked, even when the request would inconvenience you. The issue with always saying "yes" to people is that when you assume such a mantle, people will expect you to wear it always, not caring how it makes you feel. Newsflash... if you keep saying "yes" to every request (even the silly ones), they won't stop. Learn to say "no" if you aren't comfortable with the request and if it's taking too much away from you. When you learn to say "no" to certain things, you'll have the time to do what you love and pursue your dreams.

5. Think outside the box

Now that you're learning how to take control of your life, know that it's a phase of exploration. It's normal to get stuck, so if you have a mental block, shake up the norm and use other options. Connect with a mentor or a close friend and reinvigorate yourself. When you have other options you can choose from, you can discover yourself more meaningfully.

6. Be content

While this might sound ironic, being content involves learning to take charge of your life and accept your present situation. This doesn't suggest settling for less or pretending you're fulfilled even when you aren't. Being contented involves appreciating what your present situation teaches you and embracing life's difficult lessons rather than resisting them.

See your path to being in control of your life like the martial art of *Jiu Jitsu*, in which fluid movement is more effective at softening blows than fighting back at your opponents. By going with the flow and embracing curiosity, you won't get distracted by your frustrations; you'll see and unlock new possibilities.

7. Try out new things

When friends propose new adventures, are you quick to turn them down? Do you know how many opportunities you might have lost because you didn't make an effort? Perhaps you have a wide range of interests you aren't exploring because you don't want to step out of your comfort zone. Well, now is the time to change that. You can lose life-changing opportunities when you don't want to try new things.

8. Take responsibility

To regain control of your life, find a balance between what you can and can't do. When you know you can do something, you take responsibility by giving 100% of yourself.

You may need to review your actions and make changes as you move forward. So, when there's an unfavorable situation, ask yourself if you're partially responsible. You aren't doing this to punish yourself but to find the pieces of the situation that are within your power to change.

From time to time, you can take inventory of your life by asking yourself these valid questions:

- *Am I managing my time wisely?*
- *Do I stick to my budget?*

- *Am I eating well?*
- *Am I fully present in schoolwork and career?*
- *Am I getting enough rest?*
- *Am I sticking to my budget?*

As you get your answers, be nice to yourself and remember that everyone fails at some point. So, it would be best to give yourself a break, knowing that life is a learning process and you'll grow. Take responsibility by making better choices from now on.

9. Be open to what your life is trying to teach you

Eventually, you will hit what you see as your breaking point. When this happens, ensure you don't resist it but, rather, embrace it. As you walk into it, know that the moments are there to illuminate what you've been missing and longing for. Instead of fighting them, embrace the lessons the challenging moments are trying to teach you. As a result, a new path will become clear and seem more possible than ever. If you allow it, certain setbacks can pave the way for a breakthrough.

10. Learn practical skills

When things feel out of control, it's normal for you to be scared. At this moment when you're trying to take control of your life, anxiety can pop up over the many fears of the *knowns and unknowns*. To mitigate these fears, you can build practical skills such as delegating, building connections and rapport with team members, and creating time to increase your efficacy and prepare you for success.

Transform Your Life and Build a New Image

You are still young; you have so many opportunities to enjoy the good things life has to offer. Unfortunately, not all teens see their lives and the world around them that way. The world is cruel, harsh, and cold to them, making them struggle in different aspects of their lives. They never enjoy what they have or see beauty in things around them.

Scientists have suggested that the main cause of success and failure in life is your self-image. Your self-image controls your life just as your brain controls your heartbeat.

Your self-image and self-esteem are closely linked; they influence each other. While your self-esteem is how you feel about yourself – whether you feel worthy or not – your self-image is how you see yourself and what you believe you're capable of.

Your self-image is woven into your mind – your subconscious mind. Your subconscious mind is responsible for thinking and gathering information. The subconscious mind is part of determining your behavior. It is where your old self-image is locked in and controls all your actions; it literally controls all results you see in life.

If your self-image tells you that you aren't capable of being friends with anyone, or you have to work extremely hard to earn a "C," then you will be getting the exact result you expected.

Are you unsure of the self-image you have at the moment? Then look at different aspects of your life. Check the results you're getting—your schoolwork, career pursuit, personal appearance, relationship with people, and position you hold in school. The results you see are the expression of your inner image.

If you have a self-image that depicts you as "a shy person," "an unorganized person," and "a failure," you'll likely act out the character you've designed. On the other hand, if your self-image depicts "I am a straight and outgoing person," "I am an organized person," and "I am a winner," you will act *that* out. The takeaway here is that your self-image is your reality.

Your subconscious mind is mostly set on autopilot. This means that when the right direction you're going in doesn't match your subconscious self or self-image, that deviation will be picked and fed to your coordination mechanism (your nervous system). As a result, your behavior changes. Self-sabotage will set in, and you'll start aligning with your negative self-image.

This knowledge changed my life during my teenage years. I had an epiphany because of this realization, and I know it can do the same for you. You can change the negative patterns by committing to transform your life and achieve your dreams.

Now, see how reshaping one's self-image works with changing the physical body. If you want to achieve a goal of losing weight to be a cheerleader, or gaining muscles to help you join the school's soccer team, you'll need to follow specific diets and regimens to achieve this. You can't eat just anything or ignore your exercise program and expect results; you need to follow the rules to see results.

It's the same with mental reshaping. You shouldn't allow thoughts to cloud your mind or stay in your comfort zone if you expect to see positive changes. You'll need to carefully choose your thoughts and expose your mind to newer ways of thinking and a positive environment.

If you want to change negative patterns, you must build a new self-image. But how do you build this new image?

To build a new self-image, imagine the kind of life you want to live. Ask yourself questions such as *What do you want to be? How do you want your life to turn out? What would you like to be known for? Who would you be if you were well-aligned with your highest self?* Keep expanding the questions to cover all areas of your life.

After pondering on the questions, follow the steps below.

Describe whom you'd like to be

Stay committed to honoring the image you have of whom you'd like to be. Think about it, see it, feel it, and put it into writing.

Act like whom you'd like to be

Don't be content to just describe it. Start acting like the person you'd like to be. Look at your description and repeatedly affirm to yourself that you're that person.

Visualize it

As you experience each day, find a time to sit and ponder in silence. It can be just five minutes daily; the idea is to let everything in your life go at that moment and start visualizing your new image. As you see your new self clearly (without distractions), feel it with all your senses.

Repeat it

What do they say about repetition? *Repetition makes perfect!*

The more you practice these steps for building your new self-image, the sooner your behaviors will align with the new you. With a new self-image, you'll start seeing yourself differently, as someone brimming with confidence and healthy self-esteem, and someone who can overcome obstacles.

Finally, when you don't give in to the inner critic within you, you can build the self-esteem and confidence needed to start *performing at your highest levels* and reach your goals faster.

CONCLUSION

When we are intentional about how we see our-selves, carry ourselves, and live, life becomes beautiful. I have enjoyed the limitless benefits of high self-esteem and confidence, so I choose to share this proven knowledge with you. Therefore, you don't have to give up if you're constantly exhausted, stressed out, lacking confidence, and suffering from poor self-esteem.

Now that you've reached this point in this book, you should find you can quickly gain confidence, raise your self-esteem, and move past this period in your life using the techniques outlined. Living a happy life and succeed-ing in our endeavors is everyone's dream. How can we achieve all these if we lack confidence? As we close, you will have etched in your mind that you are in control of your life and experiences and that low self-esteem issues are not helpful for anyone.

If life gives you lemons, don't just sit and wallow — make lemonade. So, if you don't like how you feel, make changes. To make the desired changes, you first need to understand why you feel the way you do and think the way you do. Be on the lookout for the signs of low self-esteem and how it affects you, and utilize the techniques we've discussed to increase your confidence and self-esteem.

Don't allow memories, relationships, people, or events to make you feel less confident about yourself. Always believe in yourself and never allow doubt to rule you. Be persistent and consistent with your life goals. And along this proven path, you will master self-love, build limitless confidence, and transform your life.

Finally, don't forget to give back. And the best way to do that is to help someone change their narrative just as you have. Many people languish with low self-esteem for a long time without seeking treatment, ashamed of their sentiments. By helping others, you will constantly be reminding yourself of the values you've learned and the impact of seeking help.

Life is beautiful, and a world where teenagers feel confident in themselves enough to lead a happy life with high self-esteem is possible! You need to believe the best about yourself, breathe, and LIVE.

Best wishes.

A RESPECTFUL REQUEST

I hope you enjoyed reading! Please share your story by leaving an Amazon review.

Reviews are the lifeblood of any author's career, and for a humbly independent writer like me, every review helps tremendously.

Even if it's only a sentence or two (although the longer the better!), it will be very helpful.

Please scan the below QR code to leave your review now.

Thank you.

A FREE GIFT TO
OUR READERS

For being our valued reader, we want to offer you 3 FREE books today.

What You'll Get:

✓ **11 Essential Life Skills** *Every Teen Needs to Learn Before Leaving Home*

✓ *How to* **Be A Calm Parent** *Even When Your Teens Drive You Crazy*

✓ *15 Tips to* **Build Self-Esteem and Confidence** *in Teen Boys & Girls*

Download your FREE gift here.

www.thementorbucket.com/gift-self-esteem

RECOMMENDED READ - 1

THE DBT SKILLS
WORKBOOK FOR TEENS

*Understand Your Emotions and Manage Anxiety,
Anger, and Other Negativity to Balance Your
Life for the Better*

Please go to the below URL
for more details.

www.thementorbucket.com/dbt1

RECOMMENDED READ - 2

LIFE SKILLS
FOR TEENS WORKBOOK

35+ Essentials for Winning in the Real World

(How to Cook, Manage Money, Drive a Car, and Develop Manners, Social Skills, and More)

Go to the below URL
for more details.

www.thementorbucket.com/life-skills-teens

OTHER BOOKS

Want to read more? Please go to the below URL
and check our other books.

www.thementorbucket.com/resources

www.ingramcontent.com/pod-product-compliance
Lightning Source LLC
Chambersburg PA
CBHW031526120626
46545CB00005B/2020